KU-718-033

STUDIES IN ENGLISH LITERATURE No. 29

General Editor

David Daiches

Dean of the School of English and American Studies,
University of Sussex

CHARLES DICKENS: LITTLE DORRIT

by

J. C. REID

Associate Professor of English,
University of Auckland, New Zealand

EDWARD ARNOLD (PUBLISHERS) LTD
41 Maddox Street, London W.1

823.8
DIC
REI

© J. C. REID 1967

First Published 1967

820-31
DIC
(048)
REI

104649

R ISBN 0713151080

Printed in Great Britain by
The Camelot Press Ltd., London and Southampton

(16.11.92)

Contents

General Preface

It has become increasingly clear in recent years that what both the advanced sixth-former and the university student need most by way of help in their literary studies are close critical analyses and evaluations of individual works. Generalisations about periods or authors, general chat about the Augustan Age or the Romantic Movement, have their uses; but all too often they provide merely the illusion of knowledge and understanding of literature. All too often students come up to the university under the impression that what is required of them in their English Literature courses is the referring of particular works to the appropriate generalisations about the writer or his period. Without taking up the anti-historical position of some of the American 'New Critics', we can nevertheless recognise the need for critical studies that concentrate on the work of literary art rather than on its historical background or cultural environment.

The present series is therefore designed to provide studies of individual plays, novels and groups of poems and essays, which are known to be widely studied in sixth forms and in universities. The emphasis is on clarification and evaluation; biographical and historical facts, while they may of course be referred to as helpful to an understanding of particular elements in a writer's work, will be subordinated to critical discussion. What kind of work is this? What exactly goes on here? How good is this work, and why? These are the questions which each writer will try to answer.

DAVID DAICHES

1. *The Political Dimension*

Little Dorrit is one of Dickens's last novels, following *Bleak House* and *Hard Times* and preceding *A Tale of Two Cities*, *Great Expectations* and *Our Mutual Friend*. These novels differ in many respects from his earlier ones, in which the construction is looser, the social criticism incidental, the humour more generous and relaxed, the approach more that of the popular entertainer. Dickens is now not only devoting closer attention to structure, but also expressing a view of society more broadly critical and conceived in a sardonic and ironical mood. Robert Garis (*The Dickens Theatre*, 1965) believes that in the last novels, Dickens moved from a youthful phase in which he saw the world and people as material for the celebration of the dynamism of things to one in which his inner vitality was at odds with a more mature sense of their inertia. Hence, writes Mr. Garis, 'Dickens developed a view of the world as almost totally in the grip of a gigantic conspiracy which takes myriad forms, but of which the sole effect is to thwart and stifle human freedom and the free contact between free spirits'. A less contentious view held by A. O. J. Cockshut, J. Hillis Miller and Kathleen Tillotson among others is that, as Dickens became accustomed to success, and as personal problems pressed upon him, he was progressively disillusioned with Victorian society and came to hold a less sanguine view of human nature. Instead of confining his criticism to particular abuses, he began to scrutinise the very basis of society, and even to go beyond this to examine the nature of man and of moral action.

At the same time, Dickens's successive works show a developing conscious artistry. The early novels rely greatly upon spontaneous improvisation from his enormously fecund genius, but in the later ones, he strove to attain more coherence by providing a leading theme and a tauter construction organised round more closely-woven plots and sets of recurrent images. As nine of his novels, including *Little Dorrit*, were issued serially in monthly parts and six others published in weekly magazines, the spontaneous method, supported by a general plot-outline only, suited Dickens's special genius well. Although several of his early critics thought this 'detached and desultory form of publication' vulgar and a barrier to consistency, the enthusiastic response of the public confirmed him in this practice and he became a master of it, finding it a continual stimulus. However, after five novels in this fashion, he began to feel uneasy at the picaresque looseness encouraged by the serial method. John Forster records that the problems Dickens encountered in departing from parts of his initial scheme for *Martin Chuzzlewit* 'were such, as to render him, in his subsequent stories, more bent upon constructive care at the outset, and an adherence as far as might be to any design he had formed'. In planning his novels more carefully, he was aware, perhaps, not only of his own difficulties, but also of the fact that mid-nineteenth-century critics were beginning to take the novel seriously as an artistic form and to seek in what had been regarded as popular, ephemeral writing for aesthetic elements of balance and design.

Little Dorrit came at an important stage in Dickens's development towards his most tightly constructed novel, *Great Expectations*. It retains much of his earlier conventional, old-fashioned machinery, including a complex mystery and melodramatic characters, but it is bound together by a unified purpose, linked themes and a close pattern of symbols and images. It appeared in twenty monthly parts between December 1855 and June 1857. From *Dombey and Son* onwards, Dickens's 'number-plans' for most novels devote a page to each monthly number, which comprised three or four chapters. These notes contain summaries of plot action together with queries about significant developments. He had begun by publishing his books with little, or no, advance material written. But later he tried to complete three or more numbers (up to eighteen chapters) before serial publication commenced, so that he might maintain a tighter control on the story and not be subject to the agonising pressures of improvising to the demands of deadlines. Three parts of *Little Dorrit* (up to the end of Chapter XI) were written before the first number appeared. By this time, Dickens had a clear idea of the whole shape of his story, while still having room for embellishment and expansion. The care with which he planned the details is seen from the fact that when a hostile critic in the *Edinburgh Review* alleged that the disintegration of Mrs. Clennam's house was a topical afterthought prompted by the collapse of houses in the Tottenham Court Road, Dickens indignantly replied: 'that catastrophe is carefully prepared for from the first presentation of the old house in the story, that when Rigaud . . . first enters it . . . he is beset by a mysterious fear and shuddering: that the rotten and crazy state of the house is laboriously kept before the reader, whenever the house is shown; that the way to the demolition of the man and the house together, is paved all through the book with a painful minuteness and reiterated care of preparation.'

The number-plans show that the original title of the novel was *Nobody's Fault*, a name which also appears in his Memoranda Book among 'usable titles'. But Dickens crossed it out and substituted *Little Dorrit*. Echoes of his first thought, however, occur in the narrative itself and in the chapter titles, 'Nobody's Weakness', 'Nobody's Rival', 'Nobody's State of Mind', 'Nobody's Disappearance'. Both in the number-plans and in letters to Forster, other changes can be seen taking place, notably the emergence of Little Dorrit as the central character. At first appearance, she is merely a half-seen presence in Mrs. Clennam's room, and was originally called simply 'Dorrit' up to Chapter XII. But, while Dickens was writing Number 3, he told Forster,' I can make Dorrit very strong in the story, I hope', and indeed she soon became 'Little Dorrit' and from Chapter IX began to play a significant part. According to Forster, too, 'The book took its origin from the notion he had of a leading man for a story who would bring about all the mischief in it, lay it all on Providence, and say at every fresh calamity, "Well, it's a mercy, however, nobody was to blame, you know." ' This catalytic character does not appear in the book, but the idea he embodies is subsumed in the dominant concept of 'nobody's fault' being 'everybody's fault'. Then, having written the opening chapters, Dickens began to doubt their effectiveness and considered recasting them to achieve a different effect. 'It struck me', he told Forster, 'that it would be a new thing to show people coming together, in a chance way, as fellow travellers, and being in the same place, ignorant of one another, as happens in life; and to connect them afterwards, and make the waiting for that connection a part of the interest.' He changed his mind again, and the characters make contact in the early chapters. But some trace of the notion remains in the opening of Book II, where the reader is not given the names of the travellers who meet in the Swiss monastery and must deduce them from their speech and mannerisms. The care that Dickens gave to the construction of *Little Dorrit* demonstrates his increasing concern for formal integrity.

The immediate occasion of the book was a political one. For some time, Dickens had been publishing attacks on the Government in his magazine, *Household Words*. In the 1850's when popular demand for increasing efficiency in the Civil Service was rising, he directed his criticism more specifically against the administrative departments. Unlike several of his contemporaries, he was not opposed on principle to the centralisation of administration, but mainly to the lack of co-ordination that led to muddle, inefficiency and human misery. In 1855, Austen Henry Layard, a fiery liberal M.P. and a friend of Dickens, having seen at first hand the appalling results of the ineptitude of the British administration in the Crimean War, enlisted Dickens's help in a drive for reform. In June 1855, after Layard's motion for Civil Service reform had been overwhelmingly defeated in Parliament, the Administrative Reform Association was founded to whip up public interest in the cause. Dickens became a subscribing member and took the chair at a meeting of the Association at Drury Lane on June 27, delivering one of his best public speeches. Thus the satire of the Circumlocution Office proceeded from a vital topical issue in which Dickens was deeply involved. The extent and vehemence of his criticism of the Civil Service give the book a more precise political orientation than his other novels have. Still, it cannot be said that the political motif dominates. While he directly attacks Government administration in his periodical articles, in the novel he uses it as one type of human weakness among several, and extends his satire to include English society as a whole.

Yet *Little Dorrit* is a typical example of Dicken's constant practice of reaching back into his own past. The England he principally writes of was already a vanished England. His past rather than the present acted dynamically on his creative imagination; one of his driving impulses was a nostalgia for what he felt to be more humane, more happily individual days, which is often at odds with his reformer's concern with the present. Thus then and now are frequently blended, confused, interwoven in the novels. *Little Dorrit* is more exactly dated than most. The very first phrase, 'Thirty years ago' locates the action in the 1820's and the sense of the past is reinforced by several references throughout, e.g. 'the Palace Court, at that time one of a considerable list of everlasting bulwarks to the dignity and safety of Albion, whose places know them no more' (I, VII) and 'a one-horse carriage, irreverently called at that period of English history, a pill-box' (I, XXXIII). The Marshalsea which broods over the novel was the prison in which his father, John Dickens, was incarcerated for three months for debt in 1824, a happening which, as with his own period in a blacking-factory, was a continual source of shame for Dickens. Like Dorrit, John Dickens was released from the Marshalsea when a legacy enabled him to discharge his debts. In response to the nagging humiliation of this episode, Dickens reverts to the Marshalsea in *Pickwick Papers* and *Little Dorrit*. But by the time he wrote the latter novel, imprisonment for debt had been abolished and the Marshalsea abandoned. In his preface, he tells how, when he had finished the book, he went back to look at its ruins and was surprised to find how close the reality was to his memory of it.

The location of the novel in the 1820's makes the satire on the Circumlocution Office anachronistic, for the particular kind of inefficiency and ineptitude criticised therein belongs to the middle 1850's. Again, the arch-swindler, Merdle, as Dickens indicates in his preface, was based upon John Sadleir, the Tipperary banker, who killed himself in 1856. 'I had the general idea', he told Forster, while writing the sixth number, 'of the Society business before the Sadleir affair, but I shaped Mr. Merdle himself out of that precious rascality.' The mania for speculation, the development of joint stock companies, the rise of the 'financial wizard', all belong to the 1840's and 1850's. So, too, the picture of a London Sunday at the beginning of Chapter III, Book I, shows Dickens's reaction to Lord Robert Grosvenor's Bill enforcing rigid Sunday observance which had led to three days of public rioting in Hyde Park in June 1855.

Hence *Little Dorrit* blends social actualities of its stated period with issues that were topical when it was written. Humphry House's rule for assessing the historical importance of the novels applies exactly to this book: 'Whatever may be the imaginary date of the plot, the material most likely to be contemporary with the time of writing, and most topical to it, is the "Reformism" and the more deliberate social satire.' Dickens's social criticism suffered from his impatience with the detail of politics and from his tendency to project his personal tensions on to society in general. Yet readers, then and now, have accepted this fusion of past historical occasions with satire on current ills because, while recognising the effectiveness of Dickens's topical satire, they also recognise that he transcends the occasion, writing of the frustrations of the ordinary man at any period faced with the impersonality of Government machinery and also using the specific bureaucratic instance as one of a set of parables on the permanent defects in human nature.

The importance Dickens himself attached to the political element in the book, however, is indicated by the cover picture for the parts of the novel, which is reproduced in *Dickens at Work*. These covers, mostly drawn by 'Phiz' (H. K. Browne) to Dickens's detailed instructions, nearly always feature specific scenes and characters from the story 'shadowing out its drift and bearing', but presented in a semi-allegorical style, partly to prevent readers anticipating the 'secrets' of the plot. *Little Dorrit*'s cover is unusually allegorical. The importance of Little Dorrit herself is indicated by the sketch of her in a shaft of light outside the Marshalsea gate, placed in the centre of the design. Mrs. Clennam in her wheel-chair with Flintwich at hand are the only two other identifiable characters. For the rest, a crumbling castle on the left symbolises the world and on the right a gloomy church represents religion. Below, a frieze of jostling figures, laden with luggage and going in different directions, refers to 'life's journey' and the novel's Continental episodes. Topping the design is an emblematic cartoon featuring the Circumlocution Office and described by the *Edinburgh Review* as a picture 'representing Britannia in a bath-chair, drawn by a set of effete idiots, an old woman, a worn-out cripple in a military uniform, and a supercilious young dandy. . . . The chair is pushed on behind by six men in foolscaps, who are followed by a crowd of all ages and both sexes, intended we presume, to represent [a] universal system of jobbery and favouritism.'

Many of Dickens's contemporaries reacted sharply against the political dimension thus signalled. Anthony Trollope, a successful Post Office official, considered the Circumlocution Office satire grossly unfair. Fitzjames Stephen, the son of Sir James Stephen, an important civil servant, wrote the *Edinburgh Review* piece already quoted. He considered Mr. Tite Barnacle to be a malicious caricature of his father and the Circumlocution Office a vile parody of a worthy institution to which he had devoted his life. Stephen's criticism stung Dickens to the reply in *Household Words* on August 1, 1857, in which he protested against the reviewer's assumption that Government departments should be exempt from criticism. But while Dickens's reply is reasonable enough, Stephen had scored some palpable hits against the political tone of *Little Dorrit*; for instance, 'Dickens seems, as a general rule, to get his first notion of an abuse from the discussions which accompany its removal . . . in the present instance, he has attacked an abuse which never existed to anything like the extent he describes.' In fact, it was a constant weakness in Dickens's political criticism that he distrusted Parliament completely, and had lost faith in the possibility of reform through it, but had no clear idea what was to take its place. His ideal England, as G. M. Young writes, 'is to be built by some magic of goodwill over-riding the egoism of progress; not by law, and most emphatically not by logic'. His notions of reform were rooted in his conviction that all decent, right-thinking men, without vested interests, wished for the same changes as he did. He was impatient with, and ignorant of, details of social and political organisation. He tended to follow reformist tendencies rather than to lead them, and he was often unfair and misguided in his political judgments. But he did develop some awareness of the complexity of social forces, as his last novels show, from his earlier rather simple trust in personal initiative and the universal panacea of goodwill. He recognised, if vaguely, the movement of his age towards collectivism and the changes in social values and organisation that made it imperative. His attacks on abuses are of greatest significance when they are broad enough to deal with the obstacles between public opinion and the executive; those obstacles, in Humphry House's words, are of two main kinds, 'the degrading business of Parliamentary elections and political graft in general', and 'the sinister interests of sections of society'. That is, his basic criticism is a moral rather than a political one. In his attack on the Civil Service in *Little Dorrit* there is exaggeration, burlesque and calculated caricature prompted by genuine indignation. But its lasting value lies not in its reformist response to a topical situation or in its political awareness, but in its pointing beyond government muddle to human weaknesses, the sense of patronage, the indifference to suffering, the thoughtless as well as the conscious cruelty beneath the smooth social surface. In the context of the whole book, the political elements become subordinate to his moral criticism, his plea for charity and understanding, his sense of the restriction of human freedom by society and its institutions when the wrong people are in charge.

2. *Structure and Plot*

Dickens's mature novels are not predominantly realistic, but fuse realistic elements, satirical and comic stylisation, symbolic use of melodrama and poetic heightening into a highly personal vision of the human condition. *Little Dorrit* moves towards that form called the meta-novel, which, by its use of symbol and imagery, its complexity of significance, and its several levels of meaning, approaches the nature of poetry. In this respect, *Little Dorrit* is closer to the novels of Melville, Dostoievsky and Patrick White than to those of Thackeray, George Eliot or Trollope. In meta-novels, characters may be reduced to two-dimensional representations of abstract ideas or at least may manifest only such attributes as are relevant to a particular pattern and interact with each other so as to represent the body of mankind or society rather than a congeries of individuals. *Little Dorrit* is an organic unity assimilating diverse material, as *Moby Dick* absorbs its cetology and *Voss* its aborigine dream-world, and resembling fable or myth rather than traditional English realistic fiction. Not only are the iterated images and symbols of such novels of great importance, but the characters at times approach very close to the typical. In *Little Dorrit*, Dickens goes farther than most meta-novelists, by having both such characters as Mrs. Gowan and Mrs. General to embody particular social attitudes, and others named merely Bar, Bishop, Treasury, Admiralty, Bench. Instead of reminding us, as his characters often do, of the oddities and eccentrics of 'humours' comedies, these characters recall the old morality plays, or the satirical comedies of Molière. As Raymond Williams puts it, the real action of a Dickens novel is 'a moral action which is also a social action; a dramatisation of values and ways of living'. Dramatisation of values is, in fact, the method of *Little Dorrit*.

This method is not impaired by the fact that Dickens is imaginatively wedded to the old-fashioned type of melodramatic plot, the complex story centred on a mystery, a suppressed will or a concealed wrong. In the later novels, he puts the tangle of mystery and disclosure at the service of parable, as earlier he had used melodrama for its own sake. The villainies of Mulberry Hawk and of Jonas Chuzzlewit have their own justification as thriller elements, as do the mystery of Oliver Twist's parentage and the identity of the Single Gentleman. But later, mystery and melodrama, while retaining, of course, their 'story' qualities, acquire a new significance as vehicles for Dickens's social and moral comment. Instead of being a mere narrative device of the 'artificial' novel, the relationship of characters in the complex plot indicates the nuances of relationship between members of the same society and their moral responsibilities towards each other, no less real because they are concealed by the social structure. The change in Dickens's use of such material may be illustrated by comparing, for instance, his treatment of the Marshalsea in *Pickwick Papers* as another stage in Mr. Pickwick's miscellaneous adventures with the way in which the same prison becomes a major symbol in *Little Dorrit* and one only of the various types of prison with which the story deals.

The traditional plot material in *Little Dorrit* is embarrassing only if the novel is read as a realistic one, which it is not. Dickens retains his fondness for such elements, partly because they admit of broad emotional effects and also because he seems to take a special pleasure in manipulating them for a more sophisticated purpose. There are clear relics of the older type of novel in *Little Dorrit*. Rigaud is the stock foreign villain of melodrama, as, to some degree, Mrs. Merdle is the stock 'society matron' of stage plays. The 'inset story' employed in *Pickwick Papers* with scant relevance to the main action, is represented in *Little Dorrit* by Miss Wade's narration 'The History of a Self-Tormentor'. But again, Dickens's changed attitude towards his conventions is seen in his comment to Forster, 'In Miss Wade, I had an idea, which I thought a new one, of making the introduced story so fit into surroundings impossible of separation from the main story, as to make the life-blood of the book circulate through both.' The sentimental features of *Little Dorrit* concerning, for instance, the Plornishes, Maggy and Little Dorrit herself, are also of the kind we would find in popular fiction, although even these are presented in a different light. But there is much less of the sentimental in this novel than usual. In particular, there is no death of a child. This Victorian plot-element, which for Dickens carried a deep personal significance, he often uses to dramatise feelingly society's neglect of children. In *Little Dorrit*, he is too immediately concerned with social satire to have space for this. So, too, the poor whom he often portrays as suffering or pitiful, like the brick-maker's family in *Bleak House*, have in *Little Dorrit* a Cockney realism and are only lightly touched with sentimentality. Although Mr. Plornish, at the end of I, XII, complains of the sufferings of the poor, the very vitality of his telling and his refusal to go 'mollancholly mad' dilute the complaint, and the picture of the Plornishes at home in I, XXXI is one of the few scenes of family warmth and gaiety in a book short on such elements.

Little Dorrit is organised so as to provide as comprehensive a view of society as possible through a complex interweaving of groups of characters illustrating the intricacy of man's social and personal relationships. There is a plot-pattern, of course, and mysteries to be revealed—Clennam's real parentage, Mrs. Clennam's crime, how Old Dorrit came to the Marshalsea, Rigaud's hold on Mrs. Clennam, for instance, but the plot is pushed so far into the background and the emphasis falls so consistently on social relations and attitudes that John Wain can claim that this is Dickens's most static novel. I believe that Mr. Wain exaggerates. It is true that sometimes the main action seems to halt while we explore the Merdle or Casby household, John Chivery's hopeless love, or Mrs. General's social formulas, and that there is little orthodox narrative adventure. Yet, as always in Dickens, the novel is underpinned by a firm narrative structure. The larger pattern is a simple one: Book I, Poverty, contrasted with Book II, Riches. In the first, the Dorrits are poor, but rise to wealth; in Book II they start rich and end poor. Little Dorrit resumes the humble dress in which we first met her. Clennam begins well-to-do at the start of the novel, and, losing his money in Book II, ends on Amy's level. But within this simple up-to-riches-and-down-again pattern there are seven major areas of interest. The first deals with the Dorrit family—Old Dorrit, long-time 'Father' of the Marshalsea, his children, Amy, 'Little Dorrit', who lovingly supports him, the snobbish Fanny and his irresponsible son, Tip, both the latter corrupted by the old man's myth of gentility. Fanny, arrogant in her class-hatred, marries the foolish Sparkler, son of Mrs. Merdle; Tip becomes a hopeless waster. The second area concerns the Clennam household. Arthur returns after years abroad to the gloomy London house in which his mother has immured herself, attended by her servant, Flintwinch, and his wife, Affery. Arthur feels himself will-less and impotent; he is also haunted by the feeling that his mother's state of mind proceeds from guilt at some crime. The third area deals with the Merdles—Merdle, the great financier, courted by society, finally exposed as a swindler, his wife, the snobbish 'Bosom' and her son, Sparkler. The next area is that of the Circumlocution Office, the Government department expert in the art of How Not to Do It, a nepotic haven for the Barnacle family, which frustrates the inventor Daniel Doyce, and loses the papers relevant to Old Dorrit's case. The fifth area concerns Casby, the fake patriarch, landlord of Bleeding Heart Yard, his daughter Flora, once engaged to Clennam, and his agent Pancks, who finally rebels against Casby. The sixth centres on the Meagles family; Mr. Meagles, the retired banker, his wife and their spoiled daughter, Pet, and their servant Tattycoram, whom they drive to the arms of Miss Wade through their patronising. The seventh takes in the inhabitants of Bleeding Heart Yard, the Plornishes, Doyce, who becomes Clennam's business partner, and Cavalletto.

These are the major fields of action in the novel, in which things happen, like wooings and weddings, imprisonments and release, intrigue and revelations. The structure is like a spider's web, with many criss-crossings. Each main strand is joined at several spots by other lesser strands and thickened out with subsidiary material. For instance, the devotion of John Chivery to Amy is confined to the Marshalsea area, Mrs. General's confined to that of the wealthy Dorrits, Maggy is seen only in relation to Little Dorrit, Mr. F.'s Aunt to the Casbys. But other areas are brought into closer relationship as the novel proceeds. The Dorrits, when they acquire money, mix with the Merdle group. Old Dorrit is connected with the Clennams through Mrs. Clennam's crime and Arthur's interest in Amy. Clennam and Doyce locate their business in Bleeding Heart Yard whose landlord is Casby and where Cavalletto, Rigaud's former associate, lives; Pancks, Casby's rent-collector, is responsible both for Dorrit's gaining wealth and for the ruin of Doyce and Clennam; Miss Wade, who seduces Tattycoram from the Meagles, becomes the repository for the papers Rigaud uses to blackmail Mrs. Clennam; Henry Gowan, a relative of the Barnacles, marries Pet who is loved by Arthur; Merdle's frauds affect several of the major characters, and so on.

At the same time as he intensifies the reader's interest by such linkages, Dickens covers a wide range of social groups—the governing classes (the Barnacles); the professional classes (Bar, Church, Haggage), the financial world (Merdle, Meagles, Mrs. Clennam); and their hangers-on (Mrs. General, Rugg, Casby); the idle rich (Sparkler, Mrs. Merdle), the decayed middle class (the Dorrits, the Gowans); the world of entertainment

(Fred Dorrit, Fanny), the criminal classes (Rigaud, Cavalletto), the labourers (Plornish), the servants (Affery, Flintwinch) and a variety of occupations; Tinkler, valet; Mrs. Bangham, charwoman; Mrs. Tickit, cook; Wobbler, clerk. While the picture is not comprehensive, the general effect is of a panoramic view of English society and a demonstration of its corporate nature, with its common moral and social obligations, so that vibrations of an action on one level are felt at several others; the indifference and inefficiency of the Circumlocution Office affects the Dorrits, conversely Pancks's investigations elevate the Dorrits who affect society. The System and its workings, its hidden connections, are dramatised through the plot.

In disposing the details of his story to keep interest alive, Dickens shows great skill. The first chapter introduces Rigaud and Cavalletto. It is not until I, XXIX that Rigaud enters the lives of the main characters when he presents himself at Mrs. Clennam's house. But Dickens makes sure that we do not lose sight of him by inserting Chapter XI in which Cavalletto encounters Rigaud again and flees from him. Our awareness of Rigaud is maintained by letting Cavalletto play his part in Chapters XIII and XXV. At the beginning of Book II, Rigaud comes prominently into view, occupying a major part of six of the first ten chapters and thus preparing us for the emphais placed upon him at the end of the book. More important is Clennam's role as the real binding thread of the novel. He appears in twenty-four of the thirty-six chapters of Book I and through him we meet many of the main characters. Amy herself is not strongly established until Chapters VI and VII. After this, her part in Book I is subordinate to that of Clennam, and while her character is developed, it is he who carries the plot along. But the beginning of Book II is Little Dorrit's. Clennam does not appear in person until Chapter VIII. From then onwards these two share the interest between them. The emphasis is nicely judged. Having learnt much of Clennam, a largely negative force, in Book I, we learn more of Amy, the positive force, in Book II. So, too, Dickens carefully adjusts the introduction of major features of interest to the need for continual stimulus of his readers and balance in the whole novel. The five major locations are Mrs. Clennam's house, introduced in Chapter III, the Marshalsea, introduced in Chapter V, the Circumlocution Office, introduced in Chapter X, Bleeding Heart Yard, introduced in Chapter XII, and the Merdle house, introduced in Chapters XX and XXI. The presentation of each new location re-energises the novel. Dickens renews interest at the beginning of Book II by placing now familiar characters in Continental settings.

So it is with the introduction of important characters. Dickens gave close attention to this aspect of his novels, marking various possibilities of appropriate presentation in his number-plans. In *Little Dorrit,* he plants three separate groups in the first three chapters, and the Marshalsea group in Chapter V. But other important characters who enliven the story appear as interjections in the main narrative—Fred Dorrit in Chapter VII, Maggy in Chapter IX, Henry Gowan in Chapter XVII, Sparkler in Chapter XX, the Ruggs in Chapter XXV, Mrs. Gowan in Chapter XXVI. Then, in Book II, he concentrates on developing the intricate relationships between his large cast of some fifty-five characters. The only important new character in the second book is the formidable Mrs. General.

Characters are continually manipulated throughout, as in Shakespeare's plays, to give unity through contrast. Amy, as the main positive value in the book, contrasts, in her goodness and self-sacrifice, with the wilfulness of Fanny, the irresponsibility of Tip, the self-pitying egotism of her father, the arrogance of Mrs. Gowan and the snobbery of Mrs. Merdle; the Meagles's over-indulgence of Minnie contrasts with Old Dorrit's neglect of Amy; the evil of Rigaud with the goodwill of Cavalletto; the drive of Doyce with the apathy of Clennam; the cheerfulness in poverty of the Plornishes with the gloom in wealth of the Merdles. Further unity is provided by the many intimations of later happenings in the first part of the book. For instance, in Chapter VIII, Clennam is accidentally locked in the Marshalsea and forced to spend the night there. This prepares us for his later incarceration in the prison, after the collapse of Merdle's empire. Affery's 'dream' of seeing Flintwinch talking to his 'Double' in Chapter IV looks forward to Blandois's disclosure in II, XXX that he received the papers from Ephraim Flintwinch. Mrs. Clennam's softening in I, XXIX towards Amy prepares us for her act of reparation at the end. At the conclusion of Book I, Clennam carries Amy out of the Marshalsea in her old worn dress; at the end of Book II, in the old dress once more, she conducts him out of prison. The chance meeting of travellers at the beginning of Book I is repeated at the beginning of Book II.

Such designing produces a much more complex and developing plot than Mr. Wain admits. Yet it is true that the general effect is less of a plot in constant evolution than of a radiation out from central themes. The novel has its calculated moments of rest, and also its *longueurs*—there is too much of Rigaud's nose and moustaches and of Mr. Merdle's complaint, Flintwinch's discourse at the end is over-lengthy and dull, Pancks sometimes becomes tiresome. In the static portions involving these characters and others, we see the effect of Dickens's grappling with a much more demanding form and themes than he had tackled before; the energy which once went into exuberant humour and gratuitous detail to some extent goes now into creating a magnificently articulated fable. This kind of richly diverse yet well-ordered plan in a novel gave nineteenth-century readers much pleasure. And even today, when the relationships seem unnaturally contrived, if seen with modern realistic prejudices, its formulation merits admiration on the purely mechanical level. However, it is not the machinery that matters finally, but what Dickens used it for. The interlocking of destinies, the coincidental meetings, the hidden relationships are justified as constituting a parable of a rigidly organised society which demonstrates that all men are members one of the other.

In *Little Dorrit* Dickens employs a wide range of his normal narrative techniques, of which the dramatic one is especially important. The theatrical quality of his genius impelled him to order fiction more dramatically than most of his contemporaries. From his first novel onwards, scenes are conceived of as short plays or dramatic episodes, with stage dialogue, tensions between characters moving towards a climax, and stage-directions so complete that the scenes could be acted out with little further direction. Much of *Little Dorrit* is in this form, with scene sometimes directly leading into scene as in a Victorian play. In Chapter XXXI, for example, we have the episode where Amy calls on the Plornishes and offers to accompany Old Nandy, dressed in his workhouse uniform, to the Marshalsea to 'pay his respects' to William Dorrit. The next scene shows them meeting Fanny on the way. Fanny berates Amy for shaming the family by escorting 'a Pauper' and the scene ends with Fanny bouncing off. Amy and Nandy continue to the Marshalsea, where Amy leaves him below while she participates in a triangular dialogue with Fanny and her father, climaxed by Dorrit's 'I have seen my child, my own child, my own daughter, coming into this College out of the public streets—smiling! smiling!—arm-in-arm with—O my God, a livery!!' At this point, as in a play, John Chivery knocks at the door to announce a coming visit from Clennam. Old Dorrit's mood changes with the banknote sent by Arthur. He invites Nandy up and the next scene shows the Dorrits sharing tea with the old man, while William patronises him. Enter Tip, who sulks and insults Clennam for not having lent him money. Old Dorrit remonstrates with him, Tip stalks out and the scene ends with Old Dorrit leaving Amy and Arthur together.

These Nandy scenes form, in fact, a short play superbly dramatising the snobbery of the Dorrits and their patronising of one less fortunate than themselves; as in a play, the points are made through action and dialogue, not through interior exploration. Not only do the characters come and go on sets and play their scenes together as on a stage, but explicit stage-directions indicate their stance, gestures and movements, all reminding us that Dickens was able easily to adapt large sections of his novels for his dramatised public readings: ' "Hush, Amy", said the father, passing his pocket-handkerchief several times across his face and then grasping it convulsively in the hand that dropped across his knee'; 'The Father of the Marshalsea in the meantime took his younger daughter to his breast and patted her head'; 'Little Dorrit dutifully rose and obeyed: only pausing for a moment as she went out of the room, to give her sister a kiss of reconciliation.'

Many other scenes have a similar pattern of stage presentation, such as the splendid episode in which Fanny takes Amy to visit Mrs. Merdle in Chapter XX. Here the scene of the 'spacious semicircular drawing-room' is set with care and with emphasis on the parrot who is to act as a cynical chorus throughout the dialogue. Mrs. Merdle makes a completely theatrical entrance through a curtain: '(Amy) would have asked a question, but that Fanny with a warning frown pointed to a curtained doorway of communication with another room. The curtain shook next moment, and a lady, raising it with a heavily ringed hand, dropped it behind her again as she entered.' Several of the high emotional portions of the novel receive a theatrical treatment; for instance II, XXVII, in which John Chivery, after elaborate fencing and mystification, comes to the point by telling Clennam that Amy loves him. This is climaxed in terms of contemporary theatrical performance: ' "You," said John. And touched him with the back of his hand upon the breast, and backed to his chair, and sat down in it with a pale face, holding the arms, and shaking his head at him.

'If he had dealt Clennam a heavy blow, instead of laying that light touch upon him, its effect could not have been to shake him more. He stood amazed; his eyes looking at John; his lips parted, and seeming now and then to form the word "Me!" without uttering it; his hands dropped at his side: his whole appearance that of a man who had been awakened from sleep, and stupified by intelligence beyond his full comprehension.

' "Me!" he at length said aloud.'

Theatrical in a different way is the scene of Old Dorrit's death at Mrs. Merdle's dinner-table. The rambling soliloquy in which he thinks he is back in the Marshalsea welcoming new arrivals is a magnificent actor's piece, reminiscent of character-monologues written for Irving and perhaps having behind it a memory of the 'monopolylogues' of Charles Mathews, the actor whose technique influenced Dickens's whole approach to characterisation.

Such scenes are set in passages of narration, description and exposition. The descriptions of places especially are rich in detail and imagery which particularise them and create an atmosphere harmonious with the major mood of the novel. Such is the opening description of Marseilles imprisoned in the overpowering heat, contrasting with, yet related to, the damp dark atmosphere of the prison housing Rigaud and Cavalletto. 'Like a well, like a vault, like a tomb, the prison had no knowledge of the brightness outside; and would have kept its polluted atmosphere intact, in one of the spice islands of the Indian Ocean.' So, too, the opening of Chapter III with its stark picture of a 'gloomy, close and stale' Sunday evening in London, with its locked and barred places of entertainment, leads naturally to Clennam's thoughts of the dreary Sundays of his childhood, and his mother's dingy, crumbling house. Impressionistic use of description defines the Barnacle home in Mews Street—'a hideous little street of dead walls, stables and dunghills', where the Tite-Barnacle residence is 'a squeezed house, with a ramshackle bowed front, little dingy windows'. This squalid home, 'a gentlemanly residence in the most aristocratic part of town', epitomises the Barnacles and the Circumlocution Office they control—the preferring of a 'good address' to comfort, the airless smell of Government files, the shabby affectation of it all. Such descriptions build up an impression of gloom and frustration, which is kept from being thoroughly depressing by Dickens's continual stylistic vitality. But it does tinge the mood of the book with black. When Maggy and Amy, after their encounter with the prostitute in the London streets in Chapter XIV, move homewards, the pre-dawn hour is described not in terms of birth but of death: 'There was coming day in the flaring lights, with a feebler colour in them than they would have had at another time; coming day in the universal sharpness of the air, and the ghastly dying of the night.' The gloom spreads to other cities, too. William Dorrit sees on entering Rome, 'fragments of ruinous enclosures, yawning window gap and crazy wall, deserted houses, leaking wells, broken water-tanks, spectral cypress-trees, patches of tangled vine, and the changing of the track to a long, irregular, disordered lane, where everything was crumbling away, from the unsightly buildings to the jolting road'. The dismal view which Dickens takes of his own society pervades the whole book.

One feature of Dickens's normal narrative technique is absent from *Little Dorrit*, the picaresque elements of violence and exciting action. There is nothing here like Orlick's murderous attack on Pip, Jonas Chuzzlewit's murder of Montague Tigg or Bradley Headstone's attempt to drown Eugene Wrayburn. Rigaud's crime of murder takes place outside the narrative; the most sensational things that happen are Merdle's suicide and the collapse of the Clennam house, the former naturalistic rather than melodramatic, the second well prepared for. It is a measure of Dickens's serious involvement in social themes that, instead of a murder or an assault, Merdle's financial swindles and emotional cruelty constitute the principal crimes. Even the mystery of Clennam's birth, Mrs. Clennam's crime and Rigaud's blackmailing are pushed into the background and such characters as Maggy who, in other novels, would have been treated with considerable sentimentality, here attract hardly any.

There is, too, in *Little Dorrit* much less than usual of Dickens's more boisterous humour. The humour is sardonic, edged and bitter, matching the mood of the serious portions of the book. For example, Mr. F's Aunt is in the true line of Dickensian eccentrics; her surrealistic inconsequentialities are truly funny, but they have a vehemence and a maniacal rage that is both sinister and frightening. Instead of diminishing the seriousness of the book, Dickens's humour adds an almost nightmarish dimension to his panorama of a society in the grip of snobbery, indifference, money-lust and patronage.

3. *Metaphors and Themes*

In *Little Dorrit* Dickens is only incidentally concerned with bureaucratic inefficiency and the Victorian financial structure. Among the main motifs of the novels are the corrupting effects of social attitudes, based upon snobbery, privilege and class-divisions, the constraints on the human will imposed by a society so organised, the indifference to human misery bred by class-divisions and the pursuit of money, the illusions with which men bolster up their own egos and hide their true nature from themselves and the supreme positive value of self-abnegating love. The vehicles for these themes are the plot and three principal metaphors which, from the frequency of their use and the complex significances they gain, acquire the character of symbols. As several critics have pointed out, the prison and the family are the novel's chief metaphors. To these, I would add a third, the Church, which, if not as insistent or as obvious as the other two, I think hardly less important.

The prison is, of course, one of Dickens's most common images; the psychological reasons for this are traceable to the deep-rooted shame he felt at his father's imprisonment. Nowhere, however, not even in *Great Expectations* or *A Tale of Two Cities*, does he use it with such force and power as in *Little Dorrit*. The shadow of the prison falls over the whole book. As Lionel Trilling points out, the prison is a practical instrument for the negation of man's will. And hence it is an apt metaphor for Victorian society in which man, as Dickens sees him, is hedged in by social conventions, class divisions, Government inefficiency, obsolescent traditions. But the prisons in *Little Dorrit* are not only physical and social ones; they are psychological as well. Men are prisoners of their own fears, guilts, inhibitions. The prison metaphor also allows Dickens once again to present a favourite idea that there is no essential difference between the criminality of people like Rigaud who apes the gentleman and the frauds and thefts of upper-class or middle-class ones. So, in Chapter XII, Book II, Bar, with superbly unconscious ironic effect, quotes from Gay's *Beggar's Opera*:

> 'Since laws were made for every degree
> To curb vice in others as well as in me,

I wonder we ha'n't better company
Upon Tyburn Tree!

. . . So immensely astounded was Mr. Merdle by the entrance of Bar with such a reference in his mouth, that Bar explained himself to have been quoting Gay, "Assuredly not one of our Westminister Hall authorities", said he, "but still no despicable one to a man possessing the largely practical Mr. Merdle's knowledge of the world." Mr. Merdle looked as if he thought he would say something, but subsequently looked as if he wouldn't.' The double irony here shows that Dickens knew very well what he was about.

We are introduced to the prison and its implications at the very start of Chapter I with the description of the Marseilles gaol housing Rigaud and Cavalletto. Rigaud's lording it over Cavalletto presents the theme of patronage as well, and the dominant mood of the novel is established in the paragraph beginning: 'A prison taint was on everything there. The imprisoned damps, the imprisoned men, were all deteriorated by confinement.' We are to know that prison taint well by the end of the book. Chapter II shows several of the main characters enclosed in another kind of prison, albeit a temporary one, a quarantine island in Marseilles Harbour. In Chapter III, Clennam arriving in London sees the city as a huge prison with everything 'bolted and barred', its inhabitants in want of nothing but 'a stringent policeman' and the ghosts of its former inhabitants pitying themselves for their old places of imprisonment. Through the gloom of London, we move with Arthur to Mrs. Clennam's house, itself a kind of prison with Flintwinch as jailer and Mrs. Clennam 'in prison, and in bonds here', as she herself says. Like Miss Havisham in *Great Expectations*, she has shunned the light of day. Her imprisonment is the result of her dark, grim religion, her sense of guilt for the wrong she has done to Arthur and the Dorrits and neurotic self-indulgence. Her immobility is not physical in origin, but mental, a type of hysterical paralysis, for at the end of the novel she is driven by a new sense of responsibility to leave her house to seek Little Dorrit's forgiveness.

Only after we have passed through these three prisons do we come to the Marshalsea itself, and the Dorrits. Even when, in Book II, the newly-wealthy family tour Europe, they take the prison with them. Amy sees their present existence as a dream: 'it seemed to her as if those visions of mountains and picturesque countries might melt away at any moment, and the carriage, turning some abrupt corner, bring up with a jolt at the old Marshalsea gate' (II, III) and, at another time, it 'appeared to her that this same society in which they lived, greatly resembled a superior sort of Marshalsea' (II, VII). When William Dorrit loses his reason at the dinner-party and imagines he is back in the Marshalsea, two kinds of prison, Society and the debtors' jail, become one. Even the hospitable Swiss convent in Book II has thick stone walls, heavy doors and iron gates which, Amy thinks, make it 'something like a prison'. And when Old Dorrit enquires of the Abbot if the monastic life is not felt to be limiting and monotonous, he receives the answer that Dorrit, not being used to confinement, cannot see it from the monks' point of view. Dickens is making a point at Dorrit's expense, but, in doing so, he acknowledges that, imprisonment being a state of mind, the monks are freer than the liberated Father of the Marshalsea.

The prison image is ubiquitous. The odious Mrs. Gowan lives 'by royal favour' 'in that dreary red-brick dungeon at Hampton Court', as her son says (I, XXVI); Mr. Merdle has the Chief Butler as his jailer and is always taking his own wrists into custody 'in that constabulary manner of his' (II, XII); Miss Wade is the unhappy prisoner of her own hatred and torment as Mrs. Clennam is of her guilt; Clennam remembers that, as a child, he was marched to chapel thrice each Sunday 'morally handcuffed to another boy' (I, III); wherever Tip went he 'appeared to take the prison walls with him' (I, VII); Old Dorrit is described as 'now boasting, now despairing, in either fit a captive with the jail-rot upon him, and the impurity of his prison worn into the grain of his soul' (I, XIX); the drab London houses are like 'old places of imprisonment' (I, III); in Venice the streets contain 'dungeon-like opposite tenements' (II, V). The Circumlocution Office is like a prison, too. When Clennam visits it, he 'was generally ushered into (its rooms) by its janitors much as a pickpocket might be shown into a police-office' (II, VII); when there, he passes time with 'various troublesome Convicts who were under sentence to be broken on that wheel' (II, X). Just as the Marshalsea taints man's spirit, so does the Cicumlocution Office. The privileged rulers of the Office are like callous warders of the State who, holding their clients captive of its endless procrastination, shut out charity, decent feeling and humanity as effectively as prison walls shut out light.

Among the multiple meanings of the prison metaphor some are of special importance. First, a general sense of the oppressiveness of life itself, the limitations of mortality, the weight of the world from which escape comes, perhaps only through death, or, fitfully, through love: secondly, the frustrations felt by human beings weighed down by inefficient institutions and the crushing burden of Government bureaucracy; thirdly, the constricting effects of a stratified society dominated by class conventions; finally, the self-imposed inhibitions of the individual, created by guilt, timidity, conditioning in childhood, bullying, misunderstanding. It also functions as a complex symbol, expressing a mood of confinement that cannot be precisely defined but colours the whole vision of life in the book. Of special importance are the spiritual prisons created by hatred or selfishness or greed. The great impersonal indifference of the Circumlocution Office to the inhabitants of Bleeding Heart Yard, to Doyce and Dorrit, is matched by the lack of love Miss Wade experienced as a child or the bland indifference of Old Dorrit to Amy's self-sacrificing love. And the massive selfish indifference of Society to human misery is summed up devastatingly in the reaction of the Chief Butler to the news that Merdle has killed himself:

' "Mr. Merdle is dead."

"I should wish," said the Chief Butler, "to give a month's notice."

"Mr. Merdle has destroyed himself."

"Sir," said the Chief Butler, "this is very unpleasant to the feelings of one in my position, as calculated to awaken prejudice; and I should wish to leave immediately" ' (II, XXV).

The second great binding metaphor is that of the family. In his earlier novels, Dickens delighted in depicting happy famillies and in celebrating the virtues of family unity. His ill-treated and neglected children—Oliver, David, Smike, Jo—gain much of their poignancy by being set in contrast to closely-knit, contented families. But, in *Little Dorrit*, the family has gone sour. Only the Plornishes are happy; even they have their head removed, since Old Nandy is in the poorhouse, and they lack the vitality and glow of the Peggottys. The novel is generous in misguided, indifferent, incompetent or callous parents. Indeed, as George Orwell suggested, Dickens sees even the State as a large family 'with the wrong members in control'. The Barnacles and their relatives, the Stiltstalkings, are the prototypes of the other parents, for they treat their 'children', the citizens, as irresponsibly as the real parents treat theirs.

Old Dorrit, significantly called 'the Father of the Marshalsea', does as little for his fellow inmates as the Circumlocution Office does for its charges and he is a hopelessly inadequate parent. Completely self-centred, he corrupts Tip and Fanny by his asumptions of gentility and lives like a vampire on Amy, draining her with his demands for love, care and respect. Miss Wade and Arthur Clennam both have parents who are no parents, Miss Wade a supposed 'grandmother', who neglects her, Clennam a 'mother' who renders his life grey and cheerless by denying him affection. Casby, the fake Patriarch, is a false parent both to his charges, the tenants of Bleeding Heart Yard, and to Flora, his daughter, whom he keeps, as Dorrit keeps Amy, in a state of emotional servitude. Mrs. Gowan brings up her son, Henry, as a snobbish waster. The well-intentioned Meagles, by their exaggerated solicitude for Pet, sap her will and surrender her to a loveless marriage; in so doing, they fail in their parental duty towards their maid, Tattycoram. Mrs. Merdle rears the chuckleheaded Sparkler. Little Dorrit herself is the exception to this gallery of inept parents or pseudo-parents. To Maggy, the half-witted girl, for whom she is 'Little Mother', she is continually kind and mindful of her dignity as a human being. Like the prison theme, the perverted family relations mirror the distortion of values in a corrupt society concerned with money and status, permeated with indifference, muddle-headedness and avarice. The two metaphors reinforce each other—a bad family is a prison, Society is a prison, Society is a family with the wrong people at the head; both prison and family, tightly-bound communities, negate the individual will.

A third metaphor which helps to give the novel unity is a religious one, that of the Church. Perhaps Dickens did not give this as much emphasis in *Little Dorrit* as the others for fear of alienating his readers; perhaps, too, some of the religious imagery is natural to a nineteenth-century writer and should not be forced to carry symbolic weight. Dickens's Christianity, wholly untheological, was of the emotional, intuitive order, and he seems largely to have equated it with its humanitarian ethic. He had a piety of a simple and not to be despised kind, but it was a piety to a great degree independent of churches or worship. He continually satirises evangelical humbug; his clergymen are either odious canters or meekly ineffectual. Hence, although he accepted the Anglican

Church as part of the world of benign order he loved, he appears in *Little Dorrit* to view institutional Christianity with something of the sardonic eye with which he sees the Civil Service, hinting, through his use of religious imagery in significant contexts, that the Church, too, might be yet another institution repressing men's emotions.

In the lengthy description of the Circumlocution Office in I, X, the underlying metaphor is that of the Church: 'This glorious establishment had been early in the field, when the one sublime principle involving the difficult art of governing a country, was first distinctly revealed to statesmen. It had been foremost to study that bright revelation, and to carry its shining influence through the whole of the official proceedings' . . . 'As to the minor priests and acolytes of that temple, the result of all this was that they stood divided into two classes and, down to the junior messenger, either believed in the Circumlocution Office as a heaven-born institution, that had an absolute right to do whatever it liked; or took refuge in total infidelity, and considered it a flagrant nuisance.' 'This sparkling young Barnacle took a fresh handful of papers from numbers one and three, and carried them into the sanctuary, to offer to the presiding idol of the Circumlocution Office.' These and references of a similar kind ('with the blessing of Providence upon the harvest'); indicate that the Circumlocution Office is seen by Dickens as the temple of a religion, with some pagan trappings, to be sure, but with its revelation, its priests and its ritual uncomfortably close to those of the established Church.

In Book II, Merdle is presented in a similar way. He is now a deity worshipped by the people; 'All people knew (or thought they knew) that he had made himself immensely rich; and, for that reason alone, prostrated themselves before him . . . the high priests of this worship had the man before them as a protest against their meanness. The multitude worshipped on trust—though always distinctly knowing why—but the officiators at the altar had the man habitually in view. They sat at his feasts and he sat at theirs' (XII). In Chapter XVI, Merdle is called 'the rich man, who had in a manner revised the New Testament, and already entered into the Kingdom of Heaven. . . . As he went up the stairs, people were already posted on the lower stairs, that his shadow might fall upon them when he came down. So were the sick brought out and laid in the track of the Apostle—who had *not* got into the good society, and had *not* made the money.' After Merdle's suicide, he is described as 'he, the shining wonder, the new constellation to be followed by the wise men bringing gifts, until it stopped over certain carrion at the bottom of a bath and disappeared' (XXV).

This ironical use of religious imagery is new in Dickens; normally in his novels it reinforces sentiment or noble emotion. In *Little Dorrit* it is more pervasive and subtle than his customary satire on religious cant; it presents formal religious profession as a cloak for hypocrisy and an excuse for cruelty. Young Arthur is 'marched to chapel three times on Sundays like a military deserter, morally handcuffed to another boy'. For him his mother's Bible has 'one dented ornament on the cover like the drag of a chain'. She herself is surrounded with Biblical and religious phraseology; her language echoes the bloodthirsty passages of the Old Testament; she prays that her enemies should be put to the edge of the sword; she sits at her desk as if performing on a dumb church organ. Old Dorrit is described in a similar way. He is the 'Father' (always capitalised) of the Marshalsea; there is an inescapable hint of God the Father. When he is admonishing Tip for his clumsy approach to Clennam for money, he asks, ' "Is it the part of a Christian to-hum-not to try again!" ' 'He had worked himself', says Dickens, 'into quite a religious glow and fervour.' When he leaves the prison, he seems for the consolation of the inmates, 'to walk encirlced by the legend in golden characters, "Be comforted, my people! Bear it".' When Mrs. Merdle apologises to him, it is 'incense on the altar of his dignity'. Religious references appear in other contexts. Old Casby is 'the Patriarch', Mrs. General 'tells her polite beads, Papa, Potatoes, Poultry, Prunes and Prism'; Plornish repeats Amy's address 'in a low voice, as if he were making responses in church'; 'a brilliant company shed their lustrous benediction upon Mr. Dorrit's daughter's marriage'; Mrs. Clennam 'still reversed the order of Creation, and breathed her own breath into a clay image of her Creator. Verily, verily, travellers have seen many monstrous idols in many countries; but no human eyes have ever seen more daring, gross, and shocking images of the Divine nature, than we creatures of the dust make in our own likeness, of our own bad passions' —which last words might almost be said to sum up the message of the whole book. Hence the metaphors of prison, family and religion typify the values of Victorian society, and impart to the novel a consistency of atmosphere and tone in its generally sombre picture of English life.

There is another binding force as well, the almost clinical examination of the English class system and its accompanying patronage, servility and snobbery. Nobody has surpassed Dickens in the subtle skill with which, in *Little Dorrit*, he anatomises the English vice of snobbery on all levels of society, the Englishman's love of rank and titles, his obsequiousness before position, the middle-class capacity for insult through politeness, and for asserting the ego through patronage. He treats genteel snobbery in a tone of comic irony, but always with the underlying assumption that class distinctions form one of the major ills of English life. Here he strikes at one of the basic social assumptions of his time—that money, position, breeding give some kind of human and moral superiority to the possessors. It was this feature of the novel, above any other, surely, that made Shaw call it 'a more seditious book than *Das Kapital*'.

While family and prison work as metaphors throughout, snobbery and patronising are used directly. Dickens sees the assumed superiority of one human being to another on social or financial grounds as another barrier between people, another limitation on spontaneous feeling and another affront to human dignity. As treated here, it is a further aspect of a constant theme of his—the contrast between appearance (the social veneer) and reality (the moral and human truth). Class distinctions are maintained by vested interests, like the Barnacles; and also partly by those who accept servility cheerfully, like Mr. Chivery who looks up to his prisoners, the Dorrits. Dickens's contempt for those who worship money is expressed in the opening paragraph of Chapter XII of Book II and for those who worship position in the absurd ballet danced by the faceless Bar, Bishop, etc., around Lord Decimus Tite-Barnacle and Merdle later in the same chapter. He shows how even kindly individuals can be carriers of the disease of snobbery. The good-hearted Mr. Meagles, overwhelmed with delight at meeting young Barnacle, launches into an elaborate exploration of genealogies (I, XVII). Earlier (I, XVI), Clennam has noted Meagles's patronising of Doyce and speculates significantly, 'whether there might be in the heart of this honest, affectionate and cordial Mr. Meagles any microscopic portion of the mustard-seed that had sprung up into the great tree of the Circumlocution Office'. Snobbery, in fact, spares no level of society. One variety of it is seen in Fanny Dorrit's revenge for Mrs. Merdle's patronising of her when, in I, XX, she forces the lady to relate in front of Amy how she went about rescuing her footling son, Sparkler, from entanglement with Fanny. And, of course when the Dorrits become wealthy, she carries her revenge further by forcing Mrs. Merdle to accept her as a daughter-in-law. She tells Amy what she intends to do to 'that piece of insolence'. 'I would oppose her in everything and compete with her. I would make it the business of my life. . . . One thing I could certainly do, my child: I could make her older. And I would!' (II, XIV).

The very height of entrenched privilege and the acme of patronage are found in the Barnacles whose values are reflected downwards. Here is the earliest presentation in English fiction of the 'Old Boy Network', the interlocking caste of the privileged blandly assuming a God-given right to rule, and fiercely loyal to each other. The satirical presentation of the Barnacles and the labyrinth of the Circumlocution Office (which Mark Spilka and other relate to Kafka's picture of bureaucracy in *The Trial*) is the more devastating in that the ruling caste are not shown as monsters, but as people of considerable charm, amiable and easy-going, with their upper-class drawl and mannerisms, their relaxed casualness. The horror of young Barnacle when Clennam comes to the Office: ' "Upon my soul, you mustn't come here wanting to know, you know" ', the ridiculous story Lord Decimus tells of the pears (pairs) and the dinner-table conversation of Lord Lancaster Stiltstalking are all part of Dickens's superb creation of what A. O. J. Cockshut calls 'lazy, humane, selfish, privileged people, sheltering behind a weak barricade of minutes and forms'. As Mr. Cockshut goes on to say, 'Dickens was doing something important here; he was showing how all this loveable absurdity, which he loved too perhaps, could have consequences that were harsh and irrevocable'. Powerfully protected by their social status and buttressed by the myth that Government is a mysterious ritual conducted by a priesthood, appointed by apostolic succession, the Barnacles patronise everybody.

Their attitudes have their *reductio ab absurdum* in Old Dorrit. With his 'wonderful air of benignity and patronage' and his belief that he is conferring great favours on those who pay for his comforts, he is a parody of Lord Decimus Tite-Barnacle. And as the self-importance of the Barnacles takes its toll in bad government and human misery, so Old Dorrit's takes its toll in its effects on his children. Fanny expresses her contempt for the others 'who are all on their own level, Common' and Tip accepts as due to his 'station' Clennam's obtaining his release with the same air as Stiltstalking and Mrs. Gowan despise 'the mob' (I, XXVI).

Patronage is shown as to a great extent as much the consequence of a social structure which inhibits the full flowering of the personality as it is the result of human weakness. In the prison of society, those many who are victims of the system or of the indifference or cupidity of others, are driven by the general desire for status, a human as well as a social impulse, to find someone to look down upon. Mrs. General, for instance, is able to exploit the polite codes of society by successfully posing as a superior arbiter of manners and taste. Mrs. General's idea of being a gentlewoman is observing 'correct' behaviour; her recipe, an elaborate pattern of What is Not Done, parallels the credo of the Circumlocution Office, a negative outlook which implies Dickens's view that true gentility consists in positive charity and respect for human dignity. Rigaud's ability to worm his way into society comes largely from his success in persuading others that he is a gentleman. Henry Gowan affects gentlemanly manners and, in the most polite way, destroys reputations. This form of patronage is, in fact, a product of his own sense of inferiority to those he patronises. His mother, living her fantasy as a great lady on her distant connection with the Barnacles, loftily patronises the Meagles and makes the insult worse by deliberately mispronouncing their name as 'Mickles' and referring to the family as 'those people who belong to Henry's wife'. Her arrogance so enrages the mild Meagles that he stands up to her and speaks of her 'genteel mystifications'. It is like banging his head against a stone wall. The falsity of the assumptions on which Victorian society based its regard for certain people, the vicious comedy of snobbery, the phoney mystique of class—these, as much as anything, constitute Dickens's targets in *Little Dorrit*.

4. *Characters*

Dickens usually arranges his characters in two large groups; one consisting of the predatory, unfeeling, or avaricious people who prey on, tyrannise over, neglect, persecute, or patronise the other characters, the noble, kindly, good, self-abnegating characters who embody the middle-class virtues. The theme of a 'Change of Heart' is an important one in the early novels. Such heroes as Nicholas Nickleby and Oliver Twist remain unchanged, but young Martin Chuzzlewit is purged of his arrogance in America and the miserly Scrooge becomes a benevolent patron. In the later books, where Dickens treats his characters with more pyschological subtlety, the heroes are not unchangeably good, but suffer from some moral defect which is corrected by adversity or suffering—Pip in *Great Expectations*, Eugene Wrayburn in *Our Mutual Friend*, Clennam in *Little Dorrit*. The greater psychological realism of such characters created problems of establishing the proper relationship between these and the others which are, in Edmund Wilson's phrase 'poetic simplifications which are at the same time social symbols'. One problem, indeed, in *Little Dorrit* is that of deciding how far the characters of Arthur and Amy are convincing on their own level and in relation to the fabular character of the whole book.

Dickens's usual later technique is to work in a complicated concatenation of simple characters, each forming a continuum with the others, so that together they represent the varying facets of human nature, and give us not so much a series of relationships between complex characters as a representation of the body of mankind, an organism which is at once a vision of the city and of man, a fable of humanity and society. In *Little Dorrit* the characters are seldom endowed with a complex inner life. They are brought to some semblance of life, but they are poetically simplified so that, without losing the recognisable lineaments of humanity, they represent the forces and pressures of a venal society. But *Little Dorrit* differs from the earlier novels, too, in its comparative lack of fairy-tale characters, the Fairy Godfather figures like Mr. Brownlow or Mr. Garland, or Fairy Godmothers like Betsey Trotwood, goblins like Quilp, imps like Bailey Jnr. Almost the only survival of the fairy-tale or folk-lore types in *Little Dorrit* occurs in the story of the little old lady that Amy tells Maggy allegorising her love for Clennam, and this lies outside the story proper. There is a demon figure, to be sure, a Wicked Uncle, in Rigaud, but even he is not merely a pantomime character. Lionel Trilling sees him as 'the embodiment of evil' and says, 'one of the effects of his presence is to deprive us of the comfortable, philanthropic thought that people are nothing but instruments of injustice. Because Blandois exists, prisons are necessary.' One favourite Dickens type does appear in *Little Dorrit*. This is Maggy, the twenty-eight-year-old girl with the mentality of a child of ten. Maggy, with her innocence, her goodheartedness, her fierce loyalty to Amy, is another of the 'Holy Fool' characters, like Sloppy, Toots or Tom Pinch, who, as Jack Lindsay has suggested, come from folk-lore, the child of God who, in his combination of mental inadequacy or simplicity and goodness of heart, is a reproach and a challenge to the sophisticated. Maggy, however, is a marginal character and serves mainly to demonstrate Little Dorrit's kindness and maternal warmth and to show, by contrast, that Amy is a woman, after all, with a woman's instinct and capabilities.

In the early novels, there are characters who appear briefly, seem to promise development, then are not proceeded with. In *Little Dorrit* there are hardly any of these. Mr. Cripples, the teacher of an academy for 'evening tuition' comes and goes in one chapter. Dr. Haggage, the red-faced, brandy-drinking medical scarecrow, with the other Marshalsea inmates, Jenkinson, the Circumlocution messenger, and Captain Maroon, one of Tip's creditors, are supers, essential to thicken out the world of the novel, but none demanding enlargement. There are also singularly few characters whose sole *raison d'être* is to demonstrate the author's virtuosity or the energy of his imagination. John Chivery, for instance, another example of the hopeless young lover like William Guppy, whom Dickens found funnier than modern readers do, is not merely an occasion for some of his gentler humour and pathos, but in his touching selflessness he offers another example of the novel's positive values.

There are, of course, the typical Dickens 'humours' characters, marked by a repeated phrase or a physical characteristic—'Tugboat' Pancks, Mrs. Merdle 'the Bosom' with her pose of being a child of nature, Mr. Meagles's 'practical', Dorrit's 'ha's' and 'hum's' and so on. But all these are integrated into the story and help to delineate its themes. Some characters, used to establish the social context, are pushed to the limit of almost total abstraction, such as Bar, Bishop, Physician, Chorus and other Merdle-set characters. Even so, Dickens does characterise them, if lightly, both in their conversation and in their physical appearance. Bishop, for instance is 'crisp, fresh, cheerful, affable, bland but so surprisingly innocent;' Bar has his double eyeglass and his jury stoop. Some of his cast, conceived in comic terms, have a sinister undertone which indicates the change in his general outlook. *Little Dorrit's* comedy of financial euphemism conceals a serious comment on Victorian values; the comedy of snobbery is likewise basically serious; the characterisation is getting close to that of a Harpagon or a Tartuffe. The mature Dickens combines the funny and the horrible-grotesque in a disturbing way—Magwitch seizing young Pip in the churchyard, the evil comedy of Silas Wegg and Mr. Venus the taxidermist in *Our Mutual Friend*, the apoplectic horror, Major Bagstock, in *Dombey and Son*, for instance. In *Little Dorrit*, several of the 'amusing' characters contain a startling amount of malice and hate in their make-up—Henry Gowan with his feline slanders, Mrs. Gowan sneering at her 'inferiors', Mr. F's Aunt, a mixture of spite and rage, a kind of classical Fury or harpy, Old Casby who, when his hair and head are cut by Pancks, emerges as a repulsive figure 'a bare-polled, goggle-eyed, big-headed lumbering personage'! Mrs. General who has hard calculation lurking under her surface proprieties, Tip, surly, sour and embittered under his idler's exterior.

The 'straight' characters are presented in a quite different way. Arthur Clennam is a hero unique in the Dickens canon. He is a study in the atrophied will, perhaps partly reflecting Dickens's mature realisation that his old instinctive energies no longer served and that he had to undertake a new approach to reality in his fiction and in his everyday life. Early in the book Arthur describes his state to Meagles (II): '"I have no will. That is to say, next to none that I can put into action now."' His supposed mother, taking her revenge on this illegitimate son of her husband, has distorted his personality by denying him affection and joy. It is her shadow that lies over his heart and that he interprets as willlessness. But, despite his declarations, despite the diffidence and uncertainty that prevent him declaring his affection for Pet Meagles, his predominant mood is less the consequence of inertia, although he thinks it is, than a sense of guilt conditioned partly by Mrs. Clennam's gloomy Calvinism and crystallising mainly in the feeling that his family has derived its money from an unjustice. Far from being driven into self-tormenting bitterness, as Miss Wade is, Arthur retains an awareness of other people and of his obligations to them. If this indeterminate sense of guilt keeps him from admitting to himself his true feelings for Amy, it drives him to put himself at the service of others, to penetrate into the Circumlocution Office on behalf of the Dorrits, to do all he can to obtain justice for Daniel Doyce. It is true that, after the Merdle crash, he voluntarily accepts imprisonment in the Marshalsea to expiate for the harm he has unwittingly done to others, as his mother inflicts on herself her own punishment for her crime. But there is a difference. In Clennam's case, the act is conscious and morally based; Mrs. Clennam's action is subconsciously determined and life-denying. Clennam is a more complex character than Dickens usually drew, in that he is seen from the inside, if to a limited extent. His creation at this stage of Dickens's life inevitably leads to speculation on how far his *tedium vitae* reflects his creator's own feelings.

Mrs. Clennam herself is one of the persecutors. But Dickens has not abandoned his trust in the Change of Heart, and at the end, this sombre woman, like Miss Havisham, is given the chance to repent, when the true evil of what she had done is brought home to her by the revelation of the blackness of Rigaud's soul. Her reward is to be spared the death that comes to Rigaud when the old house collapses. Old Dorrit is the consummate self-deceiver, a man made selfish and irresponsible partly by his own weak character and partly by his twenty-three years of imprisonment. To some extent, our estimate of Dorrit is conditioned by Amy's love for him. When he reverts at the end to his Marshalsea days, 'She was not ashamed of it or ashamed of him'. Although this tells us perhaps more of Amy than of her father ('how true the light that shed false brightness round him'), yet the fidelity of the daughter modifies our judgment on the father. Apart from Amy, Fanny is perhaps the most interesting of the Dorrit group. She is snobbish, social-climbing, patronising to Amy, self-seeking. But she has a vitality and a spirit which make her anything but unsympathetic. She is, in fact, an Angry Young Woman, in revolt against her life and circumstances and taking the only way she knows to revenge herself on life. When, after Sparkler's foolishness has made her ashamed of him, she sits in front of her toilette-table 'angrily trying to cry' (II, XIV), we feel with her. Fanny, rather than Amy, looks forward to the self-willed heroines of the later novels, like Bella Wilfer and Estella. There are two other Angry Young Women in the novel—Miss Wade and Tattycoram. Miss Wade, too, rebels against the 'swollen patronage and selfishness' of Society which she identifies with her loveless upbringing, and allows bitterness to pervert her natural feelings. Tattycoram, unconsciously patronised by the Meagles, carries her own brand of resentment which drives her into Miss Wade's arms. When she is reconciled to the Meagles again, she sees in Miss Wade 'my own self ripe—turning everything the wrong way and twisting all good into evil'. This is acceptable and probable. Miss Wade remains a lost soul, Tattycoram recognises that her way is 'madness' and life-destroying, and the Meagles are brought to realise how they had erred in their earlier attitude towards Tattycoram. But Dickens is not content to leave it at that, and in one of those lapses of literary tact that his own middle-class conscience imposed upon him, he must rub in the moral. Pointing out Amy to Tattycoram, Meagles contrasts Little Dorrit's acceptance of her lot with the maid's rebellion: '"Duty, Tattycoram. Begin it early, and do it well; and there is no antecedent to it, in any origin or station, that will tell against us with the Almighty, or with ourselves."' Contrary to Dickens's intention, this complacent finger-wagging sermon makes us feel that Tattycoram has come back from the fire into the frying-pan.

Four characters owe something of their solidity to the fact that they were suggested by real people. Old Dorrit is another look by Dickens at his improvident, pompous father who had already been seen as Wilkins Micawber. Mr. Merdle is in part a 'humours' character, the joyless man with a mysterious disease which is his conscience, but he was suggested to Dickens by John Sadleir, the Irish banker who committed suicide in 1856. While the original gives authority to his satire on financial speculations, he actualises Merdle by stressing his drabness and dull conversation and by the superb touch of having him borrow the knife with which he destroys himself. He seems less an active agent of evil than a passive instrument of the corrupt will of Society. So, too, some traits of Thackeray may have gone into the character of Henry Gowan, especially Thackeray's easy cynicism and his habit of mixing praise and deprecation. However, as Humphry House remarks, the historical value of the originals is something less than the historical value of what Dickens made of them.

Closer to Dickens's own experience is Flora Finching. When he was seventeen Dickens fell obsessively in love with Maria Beadnell, the eighteen year-old daughter of a banker. Her parents opposed the association and she broke off the relationship. Dickens treasured the memory of Maria for over twenty years; then he met her again. His delighted anticipation of recapturing his bitter-sweet adolescent feeling was shattered by the reality—a fat, voluble, giggling matron, incongruously retaining girlish archness. He lost no time in severing the new acquaintance. That Dickens should even for a moment have believed that the years would spare the Maria he knew is astonishing, even when we remember the continuing power of childhood and adolescent emotions in him. In *Little Dorrit* Maria was transformed into Flora Finching, who returns into Clennam's life as Maria did into Dickens's. She, too, is a chuckle-headed chatterer full of sentimental memories and coy mystifications, with a smell of brandy about her; she is the reality of middle-age as against the remembered young charmer. But Dickens's portrait is not harsh or cruel. Foolish Flora may be, but she has a kind and generous heart; she is a truly good person. She bears the ugly burden of Mr. F's Aunt uncomplainingly; she is tender to Amy, she accepts her awful father as Amy accepts hers and she goes out of her way to tell Amy that, thinking of herself and Clennam, ' "I don't know after all whether it wasn't all nonsense between us though pleasant at the time" '. Flora, although one of Dickens's major creations, is not essential to the substance of the novel; at the same time, she adds one more character to the several 'good' ones whom Dickens shows as exercising Christian charity. She comes fully to life as Doyce, for example, never does.

The different ways in which Dickens treats two contrasting family groups, the Barnacles and the Plornishes, show his values and his aims. The first are presented as decadent nepotists, the latter as the warm centre of cheery domestic virtues. But the exploitation of the Plornishes is perfunctory compared with the Peggottys in *David Copperfield* and, save for Mrs. Plornish, whose skill in speaking 'Italian' individualises her, they in general lack the vitality of the Barnacles. Part of this, no doubt, comes from Dickens's aim of showing the Plornishes as debilitated by the oppression of society. Mrs. Plornish has been 'made somewhat slatternly . . . by poverty; and so dragged at by poverty and the children together, that their united forces had already dragged her face into wrinkles'. But there can be no reservations about the Barnacles. Here is an absolute triumph of satirical portraiture. The Barnacles all share a class sense of position and privilege but they differ in personality; ranging from the Bertie-Woosterish Clarence Barnacle, vivacious Ferdinand, not unkindly, even helpful, but never letting down the side, to Mr. Tite-Barnacle, the 'splendid, massive, overpowering and impracticable' oracle of the family, the eminent peer Lord Decimus 'who had risen to official heights on the wings of one indignant idea', pompously impervious in his armour of patronage, and to their relatives, the Stiltstalkings, chiefly Lord Lancaster, 'the noble Refrigerator who had iced several European courts in his time', and the Gowans, including the parental Gowan who, as a 'Commissioner of nothing particular somewhere or other' 'had died at his post, his drawn salary in his hand, defending it to the last extremity'. This satirical gallery of characters ranks among the finest in the language capturing, if in caricatured form, many of the real traits of the English Establishment.

One minor character deserves a little more attention. Affery, Jeremiah's wife, like many of Dickens's characters, is a little mad. Her tendency to confuse reality and dream helps Dickens's mystifications over the strange below-stairs transactions in the Clennam house. It is not until the end of the book that we learn that the 'double' of her dreams is Ephraim Flintwinch, Jeremiah's brother. But Affery also illustrates Dickens's wide knowledge of pathological states and his use of them in building up his grotesque characters. Sir Russell Brain has drawn attention to Dickens's expert clinical eye in describing the disorders from which his creations suffered, including the paraplegia of Mrs. Clennam, the nacrolepsy of Old Dorrit, the schizophrenia of Mr. F's Aunt and the mental deficiency of Maggy, with the description of her large eyes which 'seemed to be very little affected by light and to stand unnaturally still', and which Sir Russell suggests is the first account of 'the Argyll Robertson pupil'. In Affery we have, as John Wain says 'a mind so deranged that she is inarticulate except when she can call in the aid of movement'; this is another fruit of Dickens's extraordinary knowledge of pychosomatic disorders, which justifies, as it so often does, the physical oddities of his grotesques.

Thus, in *Little Dorrit*, there is no uniform way of drawing the characters: the minor ones are largely in the 'humours' manner; of the major ones, some are theatrical, some partly humours, some formed from within. All gain fullness only when seen in relation to the total pattern of the novel. Where *Little Dorrit* may seem to fail by comparison with *Pickwick Papers* or *David Copperfield* is in the amount of independent life the characters have. Pancks, the Plornishes, Doyce, Jeremiah, Henry Gowan, Bob the turnkey and others may appear to be less spontaneous creations than characters shaped solely to fulfil a function in the larger design. This is true only if we expect this novel to be a different one from the one it is. Lionel Trilling justifies the nature of some of the characterisation when he says, 'The imagination of *Little Dorrit* is marked not so much by its powers of particularisation as by its powers of generalisation and abstraction. . . . It is an imagination akin to that which created *Piers Plowman* and *Pilgrim's Progress*.' In the light of such a view of the novel we must approach the character of Little Dorrit herself. She has been variously appraised. K. J. Fielding says of her 'She is only slightly portrayed; in fact she is rather tiresome, there is such a want of reality in her.' Others have been even less kind, finding her improbably good, patient and bloodless. Contrariwise, Lionel Trilling finds that, in the only incidentally realistic context of the novel, she is 'the Beatrice of the *Comedy*, the Paraclete in human form'. Less extremely, A. O. J. Cockshut says she is 'much nearer to some Pelagian or Rousseauist conception of natural virtue than to sanctity' and adds 'the gentleness of Little Dorrit is an artistic necessity'. In both cases, the suggestion is that Amy represents Dickens's ideal; in a parable of a venal society, of selfishness and egotism, he incarnates this ideal in a girl who is patient, loving, self-effacing, uncomplaining, the 'true light'. She is a saint of the natural virtues, a shining example of goodness in a world lighted only by her charity and that of others less absolute in their goodness, her physical 'littleness' being in contrast to her moral stature. She resembles the later heroines of Shakespeare, Marina, Perdita, Miranda, in that she serves a largely symbolic or allegorical function. However, even though the novel has its fabular quality, it has, too, its realistic detail and its psychological dimension. To be credible, Amy must have human qualities and not be merely an abstraction. So Dickens puts touches to her character that attach her more closely to the world of reality. Although her upbringing has made her retain many child-like characteristics, she has a woman's emotions. In I, XIV, when the prostitute says to Amy, ' "I should never have touched you, but I thought you were a child" ', Amy does not shrink from her, though she knows the woman's calling. ' "I am not afraid of you" ', she says ' ". . . let me speak to you as if I really were a child".' Set partly to show Amy's compassion, the scene also shows that, though she is innocent, she is not ignorant. So, too, Dickens reveals a taint in her, slight but significant. In I, XXXV, after Dorrit has come into money, she asks Clennam if her father must now pay the debts for which he has been in prison. When he says this must be done, she says it is unjust that he should have suffered so much and must pay the debts as well. ' "It seems to me hard that he should pay in life and money both".' This, writes Dickens, is 'the first speck Clennam had ever seen, it was the last speck Clennam ever saw, of the prison atmosphere upon her.'

If we accept Amy, then, as someone who has preserved the innocence of childhood into adult life, as the antithesis of Rigaud, she becomes the norm by which we measure all the other characters and something more than another sentimental Victorian heroine. But this leaves the problem of the ending. Is it merely sentimental and a moral failure? Amy nurses Clennam during his long illness in the prison; he will not declare his love for her so long as he thinks she is rich; when he finds she too has lost all her money, then, and only then, will he accept her love and offer her his own. This is sentimental and stagey only if we ignore the pressure behind the book of the concept of money as a corrupting force, and the way the novel shows caste, money and sex as inseparable in the middle-class ethos. In *Great Expectations*, Pip's expectations are social position, money and Estella, and he suffers a triple disillusionment. In *Little Dorrit* it is inevitable that Clennam should feel that his love for Amy could hardly be accepted as genuine unless there is no possibility of his being interested in her money; but, also, he knows that he had failed her by not having the courage to offer her his love when she most needed it. ' "If I had then known, and told you that I loved and honoured you, not as the poor child I used to call you, but as a woman whose true hand would raise me high above myself . . ." ' he says to her. His decision that they must part is the product of his guilt sense and impulse to expiate. His surrender to her offer of love is not only recognition that she is the stronger character but also a rejection of his former inability to trust his own feelings and of the world of corrupt cash-values. The language of this scene is that of the stage, but Dickens strengthens it and makes it consistent with Clennam's and Amy's characters, by showing that he has, in fact, failed her and that it is her moral strength that reclaims him and by making the sexual union turn on a matter of wealth or poverty. The cumulative power of the book's themes validates the scene.

However, the ending of *Little Dorrit* strikingly contrasts with Dickens's earlier happy endings. So completely has the sense of frustrated feeling and spiritual enclosure been created in the novel that the climax must be a muted one. Married in the church at the gate of the Marshalsea, they go down 'to a modest life of usefulness and happiness' not to an exuberantly vital marriage; 'inseparable and blessed' they go down to the roaring streets, 'and as they passed along in sunshine and shade the noisy and the eager, and the arrogant and the forward and the vain, fretted, and chafed, and made their usual uproar'. The world at large remains unredeemed. The only hope of happiness, apart from death, lies in settling for something modest, for something less than that for which most men aspire. There is happiness here, but it is tempered by a sad sense of inadequacy in the face of men's greed, arrogance and cruelty.

5. *Language and Style*

While Dickens's style has often been discussed in fairly general terms, not much attention has been paid to its specific features or to his extra-ordinary skill in the use of language. Indications as to how such a close examination may be carried out have been given recently in articles by Randolph Quirk (see Bibliography), to which I am indebted in several places in the following comments. Dickens possessed a remarkable verbal facility; the copiousness of his vocabulary, the originality of his phrasing, the range of his rhythms and stylistic moods, his skill in adjust-ing tone are evident. It is equally plain that he was often guilty of lapses of taste, of slipping into fustian, hollow rhetoric, sentimental and falsely 'poetic' prose and flat exposition. These elements occur in *Little Dorrit* as in his other novels. But there is infinitely more in his style to be praised than to be condemned.

Dickens was much concerned with the actual mechanism of language; again and again he indicates his overt interest in varying modes of expression. After giving us examples of Mrs. Chivery's inverted phrasing (I, XXII), such as ' "Never was like what he has been since" ', he com-ments 'An effect in the nature of an affidavit was gained for the speech by Mrs. Chivery's peculiar power of construction.' In II, XII, we find ' "I only know this much", said Ferdinand, "that he has given the Department with which I have the honour to be associated"; this sparkling young Barnacle threw off the phrase sportively, as who should say, We know all about these forms of speech, but we must keep it up, we must keep the game alive.' Dickens is also alert to the ironical and comic possibilities of semantic and phonetic manipulation. At times, this shows as mere playful word-juggling, the kind of thing we feel he 'just couldn't resist'; for instance: ' "I wished to pay my respects" (says Clennam). Mr. Casby seemed a feather's weight disappointed by the last words, having perhaps prepared himself for the visitor's wishing to pay something else' (I, XIII). 'The Barnacles were all over the world, in every direction—despatch-boxing the compass' (I, XXXIV). "A, B, C, D, DA, DE, DI, DO. Dictionary order. Dorrit. That's the name, sir?" (Pancks) (I, XXIII). 'Mrs. Merdle concurred with all her heart—or with all her art, which was exactly the same thing' (II, XV). ' "Papa is a preferable mode of address," observed Mrs. General. "Father is rather vulgar, my dear. The word Papa, besides, gives a pretty form to the lips. Papa, potatoes, poultry, prunes and prism, are all very good words for the lips" ' (II, V). But sometimes his inability to resist a double meaning leads him to errors of taste which distort our perspective on a character, as when he says of John Chivery, 'There really was a genuineness to the poor fellow, and a contrast between the hardness of his hat and the softness of his heart (albeit, perhaps, of his head, too) that was moving' (I, XVIII).

He is interested, also, in the sounds and rhythms of foreign languages. Able in French himself and knowing some Italian, Dickens gently mocks the English belief that, if you speak English emphatically and loudly enough foreigners must understand it. The inhabitants of Bleeding Heart Yard spoke to John Baptist 'in very loud voices as if he were stone deaf. They constructed sentences, by way of teaching him the language in its purity, such as were addressed by the savages to Captain Cook or by Friday to Robinson Crusoe. Mrs. Plornish was particularly ingenious in this art; and attained so much celebrity for saying "Me ope you leg well soon" that it was considered in the Yard but a very short remove indeed from speaking Italian' (I, XXV). Mr. Meagles apostrophises Marseilles thus, ' "Allong and marshong, indeed. It would be more creditable to you, I think, to let other people allong and marshong about their lawful business, instead of shutting 'em up in quarantine!" ' (I, II). John Baptist's 'Altro!' is described as 'a confirmation, an assertion, a denial, a taunt, a compliment, a joke, and fifty other things' (I, I) and Rigaud is given a series of oaths and interjections which grotesquely come literally from French, 'Holy Blue!', 'My cabbage', 'Little pig', 'My faith', and so on.

The most obvious of all Dickens's devices are the various grammatical terms and modes of speaking which both give his characters individuality and impressed them on the readers of the serial numbers. Old Dorrit's 'hum's' and 'ha's' are so distinctive that they even carry over into reports of his speech: 'Therefore, my dear, he—ha—he laid his parental injunctions upon her, to remember that she was a lady' (I, III). Equally distinctive are Mrs. Clennam's preacher's language: ' "It is easy of him to talk of reparation, fresh from journeying and junketing in foreign lands and living a life of rioting and pleasure" ' (I, V); Mr. Meagles's 'practical', Mrs. Merdle's 'Society', young Barnacle's upper-class slang

' "Egod, sir, he was Pitching into our people the other day, in the most tremendous manner" ' (I, XVII), and the inconsequential interjections of Mr. F's Aunt. Dickens is also sensitive to the ways in which a person's occupation affects his speech and his imagery. He had had much experience of Parliamentary styles when he was a reporter, and some of his best effects were obtained by his burlesquing of the wordy, fatuous speeches of M.P.s and his ingenious device of having people speak in private as if they were addressing the House. Tite-Barnacle talks to Clennam exactly as if he were dictating a departmental memorandum: ' "The question may have been, in the course of official business, referred to the Circumlocution Department for its consideration. The Department may have either originated, or confirmed, a Minute making that recommendation".' (I, X); Bar's talk is full of legal jargon: '(he) hoped he might be excused if he mentioned . . . as, what we lawyers called in our pedantic way, amicus curiae, a fact that had come by accident within his knowledge' (I, XXI) as the Bishop is of ecclesiastical cant; the surgeon who attends Cavalletto deals generously in bedside jargon and professional jocosity: ' "There's a compound fracture above the knee, and a dislocation below. They are both of a beautiful kind" ' (I, XIII). Mrs. General's companion status is mirrored in her discretionary periphrases, ' "I would not be understood to say, observe, that there is nothing to improve in Fanny" ' (II, V). Even a super like the brisk Ludgate Hill waiter has his occupational jargon: ' "Chaymaid! Gelen box num seven wish see room" ' (I, III).

This last example illustrates one of the methods Dickens used to represent spoken English. His dramatic instinct, his experience as actor and public reader and his uncanny ear made him sensitive to inflections and nuances of expression not usually registered in books. For these, he adopted several devices using ordinary typography and readily assimilable by the ordinary reader. Maggy's 'Good *she* is' (I, IX) is a simple transference of 'the pronoun in a most expressive way from herself to her little mother' but her 'Such Chicking! Oh, AIN'T it a delightful place to go and stop at!' indicates ecstatic emphasis; 'Pa-ancks the gi-ipsy' is Pancks choking over a cigar; 'Hi! Ice-say! You! Seer! Ice-say! Nice Oatel!' is a Calais tout's greeting to Clennam, Affery's 'Jere-*mi*-ah!' indicates both inflection and emphasis, and the dropping of the definite article and the use of capitals suggests the lazy, yet over-emphatic, upper-class speech of Wobbler in I, X. Parentheses denote the interrelationship of two levels of conversational activity, as when Dorrit watches Frederick descending the Marshalsea steps and talks to Chivery, "Take care, Frederick! (He is very infirm.) Mind the steps! (He is so very absent.)" ' (I, XIX). Yet such typographical devices are less common in *Little Dorrit* than the many indications of tone, speed and emphasis which have something of the style of directions for reading or acting: ' "Girl?" said Mrs. Flintwinch in a rather sharp key' (I, III); ' "Sometimes", he went on in his low, soft voice, agitated, and clearing his throat every now and again' (I, VIII); ' "Indeed I have little doubt", said Flora, running on with astonishing speed, and pointing her conversation with nothing but commas and very few of them' (I, XIII). ' "(Private) I ask your pardon, sir", said Mr. Chivery in a secret manner' (I, XXII); ' "The idea of coming along the open streets, in the broad light of day, with a Pauper!" (firing off the last word as if it were a ball from an air-gun)' (I, XXXI). "You are to understand"—snorted Pancks . . . speaking in short high-pressure blasts of sentences' (I, XXXII).

Of even greater importance is Dickens's 'linguistic criticism'. The values he attacks are mirrored in those forms of expression which are suffused with cant, hollow Biblical echoes, euphemisms, verbosity, while the 'good' characters speak a formal, stately English. On the realistic level, the fact that Oliver Twist, Pip and Amy, despite their lack of education and their slum or rural upbringing, speak orderly middle-class English instead of regional or class dialects is hard to accept, unless it is seen as one of Dickens's linguistic ways of indicating character and establishing moral values in his allegorical world. Amy's normal way of expression is both formal and self-deprecating, ' "In all these foolish thoughts of mine, which I have been so hardy as to confess to you because I know you will understand me if anybody can, and will make more allowance for me than anybody else would if you cannot—in all these thoughts there is one thought scarcely ever—never—out of my memory, and that is that I hope you sometimes, in a quiet moment, have a thought for me" ' (II, IV). Clennam and Doyce likewise speak a formal, neutral English indicating Dickens's approval of them. On the other hand, the verbal practices of the hypocritical and selfish reflect their moral state. Casby's repetitions, for instance, are explicitly made indicative of his phoney benevolence: 'When he made one of these little repetitions, sitting with his hands crossed before him, he did it with his head on one side, and a gentle smile, as if he had something in his thoughts too sweetly profound to put into words' (I, XIII). Mrs. Merdle's elaborate references to her being a 'child of nature' are ludicrously incongruous with her snobberies and pretensions. Dorrit's conversation is clotted with euphemisms for money, 'testimonials' 'required accommodation' 'begging to be excused'; he unconsciously parodies his own practice when he says to Nandy, ' "We don't call this a shilling, Nandy, you know", he said, putting one in his hand. "We call it tobacco" ' (I, XXXI). The Barnacle faction's Parliamentary utterance is stuffed with windy commonplaces. The odd syntax, parentheses and exclamations of Flintwinch reflect his personality; he says things 'with a twist, as if his words had come out of him in his own wry shape'. Dickens even indicates Flintwinch's domination of Affery linguistically: ' "I remonstrated with you," she began again, "because—" "I won't have it," said Jeremiah. "You dropped down upon me." "I dropped down upon you, then, you ill-conditioned man." Jeremiah chuckled at having forced her to adopt his phrase' (I, XV). The hollow clichés with which Merdle surrounds his financial transactions reveals their essential bogusness: ' "I do generally retain in my own hands the power of exercising some preference—people in general would be pleased to call it favour—as a sort of compliment for my care and trouble" ' (II, XVI).

Always conscious of the problems of communication and the subtleties of conversation, Dickens frequently comments on the difficulty of effective communication. One of the best examples is John Chivery's 'scouring a very prairie of wild words' in II, XXVII, when he is trying to tell Clennam that Amy loves him. Dickens says, 'Ridiculous as the incoherence of his talk was, there was yet a truthfulness in Young John's simple, sentimental character, and a sense of being wounded in some very tender respect, expressed in his burning face and in the agitation of his voice and manner, which Arthur must have been cruel to disregard' (II, XXVII). Lord Decimus is described as 'trotting, with the complacency of an idiotic elephant, among howling labyrinths of sentences which he seemed to take for high roads' (I, XXXIV). When Plornish tells his condition to Clennam; 'in a prolix, gently-growling, foolish way, did Plornish turn the tangled skein of his estate about and about, like a blind man who was trying to find some beginning or end to it' (I, XII).

The fact that Dickens himself, so conscious of tone and of communication, so quick to parody inflated language, is sometimes guilty of these vices can perhaps be explained only by areas of insensitivity related to his personal life. Yet, when he is commenting seriously on a 'straight' character, his language can be little different from that which he parodies in John Chivery's self-communings: 'O! If he had known, if he had known! If he could have seen the dagger in his hand, and the cruel wounds it struck in the faithful bleeding breast of his Little Dorrit!' (I, XXXII). He sometimes, too, presses too far beyond the occasion. Mrs. Clennam's room provokes the following: 'Which of the vast multitude of travellers, under the sun and the stars, climbing the dusty hills or toiling along the weary plains, journeying by land and journeying by sea, coming and going so strangely, to meet and to act and re-act on one another, which of the host may, with no suspicion of the journey's end, be travelling surely hither?' (I, XV). At times, also, he is unwilling to trust the reader to get his point without being violently nudged: ' "Fanny," returned Mrs. General, "has force of character and self-reliance. Amy, none." None? O Mrs. General, ask the Marshalsea stones and bars. O Mrs. General, ask the milliner who taught her to work and the dancing-master who taught her sister to Dance', etc. (II, V).

Such lapses are of small significance beside the continued vitality of most of the style and the seemingly inexhaustible technical inventiveness. Flora Finching's endless flow of speech, a brilliant device, with its paucity of punctuation, its strange leaps of association and yet its curious individual logic, is an early form of the stream of consciousness method, and a remarkably faithful depiction of a type of darting feminine mind. But possibly the most typical feature of the style of *Little Dorrit* is that which Professor Quirk has, somewhat dubiously, called 'erlebte Rede'. This is a particular type of reported speech which Quirk suggests can give narrative speed as well as suggesting a speaker's typical idiom, his unspoken reflections, and the impact of one character upon another. In *Little Dorrit* Dickens uses 'erlebte Rede' for a wide variety of effects: as conveying the lofty monarchical impersonality of Old Dorrit: 'He received them, in his poor room . . . with a kind of bowed-down beneficence. They were welcome to the Marshalsea, he would tell them. Yes, he was the Father of the place. So the world was kind enough to call him; and so he was, if more than twenty years of residence gave him a claim to that title. It looked small at first, but there was very good company there—among a mixture—necessarily a mixture—and very good air' (I, VI); or as a reflection of Mrs. Merdle's bored detachment: 'She hoped Edmund might like it, but really she didn't know. It would keep him in town a great deal, and he preferred the country. Still, it was not a disagreeable position—and it was a position' (II, XIV); or as a rendering of Plornish's confused grumble, 'He could tell you who suffered, but he couldn't tell you whose fault it was. It wasn't *his* place to find out, and who'd mind what he said, if he did find out? He only know'd that it wasn't put right by them what undertook that line of business, and that it didn't come right of itself' (I, XII). It can also indicate soul-sickness and weariness. '"You shall if you like," said Affery, "There's her tomorrow's partridge in the larder . . . say the word and I'll cook it." No, he had not long dined, and could eat nothing' (I, III).

These and many other linguistic devices show Dickens still master of language and self-assured in his virtuosity. Similarly, his use of imagery shows both his fertility and his sense of the work's unity. We have already looked at his use of the large metaphors. But many of the incidental images also contribute to the creation of a single atmospheric and symbolic impression. In tune with the book's predominant sombreness and its sense of waste and oppression, much of the imagery is of death and devastation. Mrs. Clennam's house is described largely in terms of death and deformity, since it is inhabited by twisted souls: 'the black bier-like sofa', the 'great angular black bolster, like the block at a state execution'; the staircase 'panelled off into spaces like so many mourning tablets', the old cellaret 'like a sort of coffin in compartments'; the bedroom furniture which includes 'a maimed table, a crippled wardrobe, a lean set of fire-irons like a skeleton of a set deceased . . . and a bedstead with four bare atomies of posts, each terminating in a spike as if for the dismal accommodation of lodgers who might prefer to impale themselves.' In the drawing-room is 'a pair of meagre mirrors, with dismal processions of black figures carrying black garlands, walking round the frames', and featuring 'one undertaker-like Cupid'. The entrance to the house has carved work with 'children's heads with water on the brain'. From his window, Arthur looks down on 'an old blasted and blackened forest of chimneys'. Flintwinch has a neck so twisted 'that he had a weird appearance of having hanged himself at one time or another'. But the imagery of death and decay is not confined to the Clennam house. In the sweltering Marshalsea, as Amy is born, 'the flies fell into the traps by hundreds; and at length one little life, hardly stronger than theirs, appeared among the multitude of lesser deaths'. It even adheres to Flora, since Clennam's love for her is dead. She tosses her hair 'with a caricature of her girlish manner, such as a mummer might have presented at her own funeral, if she had lived and died in classical antiquity'. Death imagery clusters around Clennam, dead of soul: 'To review his life was like descending a green tree in fruit and flower, and seeing all the branches wither and drop off one by one, as he came towards them.' Merdle sows disaster and despair: the collapse of his empire is like a disastrous sea-battle leaving 'nothing but burning hulls, bursting magazines, great guns self-exploded tearing friends and neighbours to pieces, drowning men clinging to unseaworthy spars and going down every minute, spent swimmers, floating dead, and sharks'. Images of taint and disease, used so effectively in the other later novels, likewise in *Little Dorrit* represent the infections of society. The Marshalsea is 'a well whose waters had their own peculiar stain'; the prisoners regard 'the payment of debts as a disease that occasionally broke out'; Merdle's boom is elaborately equated with the Plague in II, XIII, 'The Progress of an Epidemic'; when Pancks wants to speculate, Dickens says, 'Bred, at first, as many physical diseases are, in the wickedness of men, and then disseminated in their ignorance, these epidemics, after a period, get communicated to many sufferers who are neither ignorant nor wicked.' And various images of cold collect around the upper class, as they do around Mr. Dombey, indicating their frigidity of spirit. Lord Lancaster is a 'noble Refrigerator who had iced several European courts in his time'; his cravat is 'like a stiff snow-drift'; he ends the evening by 'freezing a cup of tea for his own drinking and retiring at his lowest temperature'. Even when the images are not of death, disease or cold, they tend to be ugly, grotesque, repulsive. Rigaud's nose is like that of a bird of prey, his cold, white hands are 'lithely twisting and twining one over another like serpents'. Mr. Tite-Barnacle's house is in a 'little dark area like a damp waistcoat-pocket'; the adjacent house is 'a fearful little coop'; the house itself is 'like a sort of bottle filled with a strong distillation of mews'. Old Dorrit opens and shuts his hands 'like valves'; Mr. Merdle oozes 'sluggishly and muddily about his drawing-room'.

Other stylistic elements play their part in shaping the atmosphere of the novel. Animism is a distinctive feature of Dickens's vision; his dynamic genius endows innumerable inanimate objects with life, making them all vibrate to his personality as part of the Dickens world. Animism is a vehicle for his constant humour, a means of dramatisation, an element which reinforces the parable character of the novels and helps to give them a non-realistic context, and a way of creating atmosphere. The elements, given personalities of their own, help to transform melodrama into symbolic action, as the fog and rain do in *Bleak House*. In *Little Dorrit*, animism is less potent than in the other later novels, perhaps because the emphasis lies so heavily on social satire. Nevertheless, it functions powerfully at times and is consistent with the novel's general character in its suggestion of debilitation and decrepitude. Houses, clothing, furniture and other possessions partake of the nature of the people owning them, share their values and incarnate Dickens's view of the social organism. In the first five paragraphs of Chapter I, the word 'stare' and its variants occur seventeen times; it is the Marseilles sun that stares and glares here, yet its insistence invites the reader to equate it with the author's eye playing over the whole of Victorian society, even its darkest corners. In the same chapter, the relationship between people and things is stated directly: 'The other man (John Baptist) spat suddenly on the pavement and gurgled in his throat. Some lock below gurgled in *its* throat immediately afterwards'; and in the next chapter Mrs. Merdle's face is described as 'a pleasant English face which had been looking at homely things for five-and-fifty years or more, and shone with a bright reflection of them'. When the physical surroundings of the characters become animate, they mirror the greyness of urban life and the drabness of soul of the city dwellers: 'Melancholy streets in a penitential garb of soot', 'ten thousand responsible houses . . . frowning as heavily on the streets they composed, as if they were every one inhabited by the ten young men of the Calendar's story, who blackened their faces and bemoaned their miseries every night'; the church bell 'which abandoned hope and shook every house . . . with one dismal swing per second, as a groan of despair'; the street lamps which one 'might have fancied astonished at being suffered to introduce any show of brightness into such a dismal scene', 'a wretched little bill Found Drowned, weeping on the wet wall', the Clennam house 'leaning on some half-dozen gigantic crutches', the 'large hard-featured clock' on the Clennam sideboard, 'which he used to see bending its figured brows upon him with a savage joy when he was behind-hand with his lessons', the 'gaunt rooms' which 'seemed to have settled down into a gloomy lethargy from which nothing could raise them again'. But it is not only the English Sunday and Mrs. Clennam's house that are animated so gloomily. 'The morning light was in no hurry to climb the prison wall and look in at the Snuggery windows'; in the streets, Clennam walks among 'waifs of straw and dust and paper'; Casby's house in Gray's Inn Road 'had set off from that thoroughfare with the intention of running at one heat down into the valley and up again to the top of Pentonville Hill, but had run itself out of breath in twenty yards, and had stood still ever since'; the theatre where Fanny works has a 'furtive sort of door, with a curious up-all-night air about it'; the area near Oxford Street is full of 'great streets of melancholy stateliness, and little streets that try to be as stately, and succeed in being more melancholy'; the Sparklers' house is at all times 'stuffed and close as if it had an incurable cold in its head'; in Mr. Rugg's garden 'a few of the dustiest of leaves hung their heads and led a life of choking'.

Yet even more significant in *Little Dorrit* is the amount of automatism, the opposite of animism, the seeing of living people as things or puppets. This reflects the concept behind the book that people are not in possession of their own wills, but are controlled by the System, by society, by Convention, by great impersonal forces. Mr. F's Aunt has a face 'like a staring wooden doll too cheap for expression, and a stiff yellow wig perched unevenly on the top of her head'; Pancks is 'the panting little steam-tug'; at the theatre, there is 'a man so much in want of airing that he had a blue mould upon him' and a woman, 'in such a tumbled condition altogether, that it seemed as if it would be an act of kindness to iron her'; in the Marshalsea, visitors and prisoners 'still lingered in corners, as broken cobwebs and such unsightly discomforts draggle in corners of other places'; in Harley Street, the mansions and their inhabitants are so much alike that the people stare 'at the other side of the way with the dullness of the houses'; Mrs. Merdle is 'a superb jewel-stand'; the Barnacles 'were dealt, by the heads of the family, like so many cards below the court-cards, to public dinners and meetings'; Flintwinch is 'a rusty screw in gaiters'; Fanny shuts up Sparkler 'like a box'; a servant-maid 'ticks two words'; Mrs. General is 'a cool, waxy, blown-out woman, who had never lighted well'; Flora is 'a statue bride'.

The cumulative effect of such images, animism and automatism is to create in this, his saddest novel, a mood of grim oppressiveness, waste and frustrated emotions against which the drama of Clennam's return to life and of Amy's self-sacrifice stand out more strikingly. One aspect of the novel that is forced upon us by the descriptions of streets and houses, of weather, rain, mud, sleet and cold, is Dickens's tremendous sense of the city, of the poetry of the city, of its beauty and its terror, of its presence. ' "London looks so large, so barren, and so wild." In Little Dorrit's eyes, its vastness under the black sky was awful.' With novels like this one, Dickens virtually invented the English novel of the city, and became, with Baudelaire, a poet of urban reality, responding creatively to the fact of the modern city, constructing a self-subsistent world from its elements, fascinated by its squalor, its diversity, its smells, sounds, sights, its effects on the souls of men, its inequalities of wealth and poverty, seeing in it a microcosm of mankind, including in his vision of it a dark Gothic strain, a haunting dark poetry. His predecessors, like Pierce Egan, who had exploited London, had done so with only a tripper's awareness of its complexity and special character, so that they wrote mainly lightly fictional guide-books. Dickens responds to it as a profound experience. Without losing his grip upon detail, absorbed in the inexhaustible richness of its humanity and its physical character, he reshapes it into a haunting landscape of the mind, amidst which his characters play out a drama of good and evil, honesty and hypocrisy, self-interest and self-sacrifice, and the venality of Victorian society is exposed in a dark fable of social drives and human weaknesses.

Select Bibliography

Novels

A Tale of Two Cities, O.U.P. (1949).
Bleak House, O.U.P. (1951).
Great Expectations, O.U.P. (1953).

Letters

The Letters of Charles Dickens, edited by Walter Dexter. 3 vols. Nonesuch Press (1938).
The Letters of Charles Dickens, edited by Madeline House and Graham Storey. Vol. 1, 1820–1839. Clarendon Press (1965).

Biography and Criticism

John Forster, *The Life of Charles Dickens* (1872–4).
George Gissing, *Charles Dickens: A Critical Study* (1903).
G. K. Chesterton, *Charles Dickens* (1906).
Edmund Wilson, *The Wound and the Bow* (1941).
Humphry House, *The Dickens World* (1941).
Una Pope-Hennessy, *Charles Dickens* (1945).
George Orwell, *Collected Essays* (1946).
R. J. Cruikshank, *Dickens and Early Victorian England* (1949).
Jack Lindsay, *Charles Dickens* (1950).
Graham Greene, *The Lost Childhood* (1950).
Lionel Trilling, *The Liberal Imagination* (1951).
— Introduction to *Little Dorrit*, O.U.P. (1953).
Edgar Johnson, *Charles Dickens: His Tragedy and Triumph*, 2 vols. (1952).
G. H. Ford, *Dickens and his Readers* (1955).
M. D. Zabel, *Craft and Character in Modern Fiction* (1957).
John Butt and Kathleen Tillotson, *Dickens at Work* (1957).
J. Hillis Miller, *Charles Dickens: The World of his Novels* (1958).
K. J. Fielding, *Charles Dickens: A Critical Introduction* (1958), 2nd ed. revised 1966.
Monroe Engel, *The Maturity of Dickens* (1959).
Randolph Quirk, *Charles Dickens and Appropriate Language*, Durham University (1959).

A. O. J. Cockshut, *The Imagination of Charles Dickens* (1961).
G. H. Ford and Lauriat Lane (eds.), *The Dickens Critics* (1961).
J. C. Reid, *The Hidden World of Charles Dickens*, Auckland University (1962).
John Gross and Gabriel Pearson, *Dickens and the Twentieth Century* (1962).
Philip Collins, *Dickens and Crime* (1962).
Mark Spilka, *Dickens and Kafka* (1963).
Earle Davis, *The Flint and the Flame* (1963).
Robert Garis, *The Dickens Theatre* (1965).

Some Articles

Fitzjames Stephen, 'The License of Modern Novelists', *Edinburgh Review*, Vol. CVI, July 1857.
Charles Dickens, 'Curious Misprint in the *Edinburgh Review*', *Household Words*, Vol. XVI, August 1, 1857.
Sir Russell Brain, 'Dickensian Diagnoses', *British Medical Journal*, December 1955.
Randolph Quirk, 'Some Observations on the Language of Charles Dickens', *Review of English Literature*, Vol. II, 1961.
John D. Jump, 'Clennam at the Circumlocution Office', *Critical Survey*, Vol. 1, 1963.
Vivien M. Bell, 'Mrs. General's Victorian England', *19th Century Fiction*, 1965.

Index

BARRY - GLAMORGAN COLLEGE OF EDUCATION
LIBRARY